This book belongs to

_____

Dedicated to our Memory Makers audience who we hope will find ultimate inspiration in the ideas to be discovered inside. A very special thanks to the 2004 Memory Makers Masters for sharing their exceptional signature styles, insights and artistry.

Associate Editor & Writer Emily Curry Hitchingham

Art Director Nick Nyffeler

Graphic Designer Robin Rozum

Art Aquisitions Editor Janetta Abucejo Wieneke

Craft Editor Jodi Amidei

Photographer Ken Trujillo

Contributing Photographers Lizzy Creazzo, Jennifer Reeves

2004 Memory Makers Masters Joanna Bolick, Jennifer Bourgeault,
Susan Cyrus, Lisa Dixon, Kathy Fesmire, Angie Head, Michelle Pesce,
Denise Tucker, Andrea Lyn Vetten-Marley, Sharon Whitehead

Editorial Support Karen Cain, MaryJo Regier, Lydia Rueger, Dena Twinem

Hand Model Ann Kitayama

Memory Makers® *Mastering Scrapbook Styles*

Published by Memory Makers Books, an imprint of F+W Publications, Inc.
12365 Huron Street, Suite 500, Denver, CO 80234
Phone 1-800-254-9124
First edition. Printed in the United States.
09 08 07 06 05 5 4 3 2 1

Library of Congress Cataloging-in-Publication Data

Mastering scrapbook styles : tips, tricks and techniques from the Memory Makers masters
/ [writer, Emily Curry Hitchingham].-- 1st ed.
    p. cm.
    Compilation of artwork from the winners of the 2004 Memory Makers masters competition.
    Contents: Transparent embellishments with Joanna Bolick -- Geometric shapes with
Jennifer Bourgeault -- Playful page themes with Susan Cyrus -- Journaling with Lisa
Dixon -- Color with Kathy Fesmire -- Interactive elements with Angie Head -- Creative
typography with Michelle Pesce -- Texture with Denise Tucker -- Sewing and notions with
Andrea Lyn Vetten-Marley -- Design details with Sharon Whitehead.
    Includes index.
    ISBN 1-892127-55-5
    1. Photograph albums. 2. Photographs--Conservation and restoration. 3. Scrapbooks. I.
Hitchingham, Emily Curry. II. Memory Makers Books.

TR465.M36 2005
745.593--dc22

                                                                            2004065556

Distributed to trade and art markets by
F+W Publications, Inc.
4700 East Galbraith Road, Cincinnati, OH 45236
Phone 1-800-289-0963

ISBN 1-892127-55-5
Memory Makers Books is the home of *Memory Makers,* the scrapbook magazine dedicated to educating and inspiring scrapbookers.
To subscribe, or for more information, call (800) 366-6465. Visit us on the Internet at www.memorymakersmagazine.com.

Introduction

For the second straight year, the month of August was marked at Memory Makers with postal bins brimming with boxes and bulky envelopes. Each day delivery trucks made increasingly extended stops as drivers unloaded more packages. Before long our reception area and editorial hallways were lined with an assortment of parcels waiting to be opened. As each wave of arrivals ushered in another, our final tally peaked just shy of 500 submissions. Following lengthy and careful consideration, it was time to select the 2004 Memory Makers Masters.

Our yearly competition to select ten top scrapbook artists is an exciting and challenging task. All of us eagerly anticipate the contest deadline and the prospect of casting our votes, knowing we will see outstanding artwork and that gifted new artists will be discovered. By seeking out this panel of cutting-edge scrapbookers, the pages of our books and magazines and the imaginations of our readers are greatly enriched.

To celebrate and share the innovation and expertise of the Masters, we have compiled this collection with the goal of making it unlike other idea resources you'll see. In addition to over 200 top-notch pages that epitomize scrapbook artistry, you'll meet each of the Masters through sections devoted entirely to each crafter's specialty, or signature style. Designed to both inspire and educate, you'll be motivated to approach essential elements of scrapbooking in all-new ways, including journaling, design, texture, color and so much more straight from these industry experts. Moreover, illustrated step-by-step projects and tips, tricks and techniques accompanying each page distinguish this book as a must-have for your collection.

We are proud to commemorate these women's contributions to our publications over the past year. They have answered our challenges and pushed the creative envelope each time we have called upon them to do so. This book is a representation of their outstanding efforts, which we are pleased to offer to you as a comprehensive crafting tool. Discover for yourself throughout these pages what sets these women apart as truly exceptional masters of their craft.

Enjoy!

Emily

Emily Curry Hitchingham, Associate Editor

Table of Contents

MASTERING...

There just seems to be something about boys and trucks. (Boys of any age, I might add!) Your Grandpa Monson has a strong affinity for old cars and trucks, and it appears he has found his companion for such pleasures in you. While we were in Minnesota for Uncle Mark's graduation you were immediately drawn to this old Studebaker sitting for extinction at the farm. I love that these photos capture a mix of both the old and the new, and are a reflection of a pastime that continues to endure. I hope you will always have opportunities to learn about the past, little boy, and appreciate those who rode before you. May 2004.

Joanna BOLICK

Transparent Embellishments

Although Joanna dabbled in scrapbooking in college, it wasn't until a work colleague invited her to a crop that she was introduced to the enticing product and artistic possibilities the hobby has to offer. After discovering the scrapbook magazine section at a local book store, Joanna says her eyes were ultimately opened to what she could do with a scrapbook page.

Because of her interests in photography and words, Joanna keeps her pages photocentric and plays with innovative ways to feature her text. In order to incorporate accents and journaling without upstaging her subject, Joanna discovered clear elements such as mica and transparencies to be the perfect solution. "I am particularly fond of using clear elements because I feel they complement the theme of the page without removing the focus from the photos themselves. I also love the fact that they add the illusion of depth to a page while keeping the page from getting too bulky...not that there's anything wrong with that!" Although extremely versatile, Joanna notes that the very transparent nature she so enjoys about clear elements can make them tricky to work with. "You have to be a little more inventive with the ways you attach them to your pages, and having the right adhesives makes all the difference."

In addition to her work as a scrapbook instructor and designer, Joanna keeps busy as a stay-at-home mom. She lives in Fletcher, North Carolina, with husband Mark and son Cole.

Love You

A bold sunflower transparency of one of Joanna's favorite photos creates impact in this page celebrating a shared moment of mother-son affection. Joanna created additional visual interest by layering the transparency with text-patterned paper and a small vellum quote.

Photo: Mark Bolick, Fletcher, North Carolina

TECHNIQUE: Create your own photo transparency in Adobe Photoshop after selecting and enlarging a photo. Choose "ink jet transparency" from the settings menu and print onto a transparency sheet.

Supplies: Patterned papers (Daisy D's); index card, letter stencil, leather letter (Autumn Leaves); bottle cap (Li'l Davis Designs); vellum quote (Memories Complete); ribbon (K & Company); image editing software (Adobe Photoshop); jump ring; transparency

A Year of You

Here Joanna utilized photo negative sleeves to showcase several favorite photos of her son. By choosing to utilize only a portion of the larger negative strip and by housing black-and-white and color photos in both, Joanna created a quick and easy, eye-pleasing arrangement.

TRICK: Joanna employed two different means of keeping her photos contained within the photo negative sleeves: a staple for the smaller strip and adhesive for the larger one.

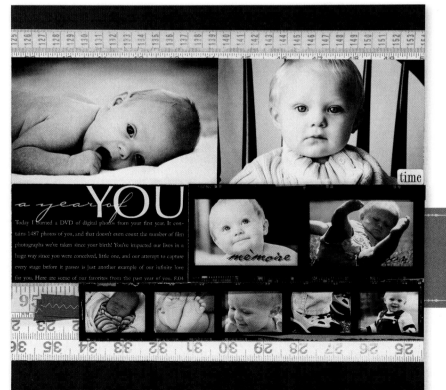

Supplies: Photo negative sleeves (Creative Imaginations); patterned paper (Rusty Pickle); "time" tag (Making Memories); ribbon (K & Company); black cardstock; staple

Majestic Fall

Vertical passage-like journaling artfully parallels Joanna's striking photo of towering autumn trees. Printing the journaling on two different transparencies and layering them one atop another helped to make the text bold when it could have easily become lost against the page background.

TRICK: Distressing the text-patterned paper through light sanding allows the transparency-printed journaling to be legible against the design.

Supplies: Patterned paper, ruler sticker (K & Company); twill sticker (Pebbles); label (Dymo); black cardstock; gold brads; transparencies

A Time to Grow

Joanna used a small safety pin to creatively attach a premade vellum quote accent to her oversized photo. Though a small detail, the addition provided an artful means of incorporating a clear element that played directly into her page theme.

TIP: Look to clear elements when all page space has been utilized with a title, photos and journaling yet the page still needs a little "something." By their clear nature, these additions may be added in numerous ways anywhere on the layout.

Supplies: Patterned paper (7 Gypsies); light brown patterned paper (Chatterbox); vellum quote (Memories Complete); rub-on words, safety pin (Making Memories); brown cardstock

Supplies: Green faux textured patterned paper (Designer's Library); textured white cardstock (Bazzill); microscope slides (VRW); wooden frame (Li'l Davis Designs); pesto-and raisin-colored alcohol inks (Ranger); quote (Quote, Unquote by Autumn Leaves); silk flower (Michael's); pink mini brads (Boxer Scrapbook Productions)

"How does one get to be a butterfly?" she asked pensively. "You must want to fly so much that you are willing to give up being a caterpillar."

- Trina Paulus

The beauty of the butterfly can be captivating. Observing the butterflies at an exhibit at the Nature Center this week served a dual purpose for me. First, the butterflies inspired me with their gorgeous designs, symmetry, and vibrant colors. Second of all, and most importantly, they also served to remind me that God's hand in each particle of life, including mine. Like the butterfly in the quote above, who must give up being a caterpillar in order to learn how to fly, I, too, must give up my old self and my selfish desires in order to follow God's will for my life. Although this is sometimes easier said than done, God is the one who knows best, and because we believe in him, we are richly blessed. For that, and for reminders of his love, I am very thankful. 8.22.04

Life's Blessings

To complement her stunning butterfly photo, Joanna used alcohol ink-treated microscope slides to form an equally striking frame. She mounted her photo and microscope slide on textured white cardstock before adhering along with faux patterned paper to the black background. This provided added structure and allowed the colors of the slides to pop.

Apply a few drops of ink directly to the surface of the slide, starting with the darker ink. Quickly spread the ink around the slide using the tip of the bottle or by tilting the slide. Note: Ink will dry quickly.

Apply the second ink while the first ink is still drying. This will allow the two colors to mix and create a unique design.

Once dry, adhere the slide to the page using a clear liquid adhesive.

Sun

Joanna added an eye-catching splash of color to this seaside layout by applying acrylic paint to the glossy side of a transparency using a foam brush. After allowing the paint to dry, she then printed her journaling in column format onto the rough side of the transparency. For a unique addition to her own words, Joanna included a segment from a printed definition transparency in keeping with the seasonal theme of her layout.

Supplies: Patterned papers (Rusty Pickle); definition (Daisy D's); paper flowers, brads, acrylic paint (Making Memories); transparency (Grafix); silk flower petals

TECHNIQUE: Dress up ordinary transparencies in a flash with custom acrylic paint designs or by combining and layering them with elements that embody your page theme.

Sweet Affection

Several creative effects were achieved with clear elements on this vibrant page. Vellum was layered over patterned paper to soften its bright hues. Joanna's precut circular mica accents feature words created in Adobe InDesign software and mimic the look of the lollipop. Finally, a clear epoxy sticker adds emphasis to the second portion of the page title.

Photo: Beth Hooper, Cedar Mountain, North Carolina

TECHNIQUE: For her journaling, Joanna first created a circle template in Adobe InDesign and used the "type of path" tool to type within the circle. She then printed the journaling onto clear inkjet transparencies and adhered them on top of or behind the mica pieces with a clear liquid adhesive.

Supplies: Patterned paper and punch-out circles (KI Memories); mica circles (USArtQuest); pink rub-ons (Scrapworks); clear epoxy sticker (SEI); textured pink cardstock (Bazzill); page layout software (Adobe InDesign); hot pink paper; vellum, transparency

Racin'

Joanna incorporated collage elements and mica fragments into this layout commemorating speed and race-against-time themes. A clock face and printed tags were layered beneath sheets of mica and secured in place with clear-drying adhesive for a unique assemblage. Joanna printed the journaling and oversized numbers onto paper, then adhered a very thin layer of mica over the journaling with nonstick tape and printed the text again. She then carefully removed the mica from the paper, making sure not to smudge the ink before immediately embossing. Joanna layered the mica sheets over the collaged elements with clear adhesive.

TIP: To easily multiply the number of mica sheets you have to work with, use a craft knife to separate the layers. Smaller 1-3" sections are easiest to work with. Mica can be cut or die cut into numerous shapes as well.

Supplies: Yellow patterned paper (Artistic Scrapper); number patterned paper (Rusty Pickle); bookmark, epoxy tiles, clock sticker (EK Success); black run-ons, mini tags (Making Memories); red rub-ons (Autumn Leaves); mica (USArtQuest); diamond glaze (JudiKins); acrylic paint; black embossing powder; staples; ticket stub; ribbon

random advice

✻ Rules for happiness: Something to do, someone to love, something to hope for. Immanuel Kant

✻ Laughter is the shortest distance between two people. Victor Borge

✻ You must always be curious. Walt Whitman

✻ To love what you do and know that it matters... how could anything be more fun? Katharine Graham

✻ Savor the moments that are warm and special and giggly. Sammy Davis Jr.

✻ Seek the wisdom of the ages, but look at the world through the eyes of a child. Ron Wild

✻ The best and most beautiful things in the world cannot be seen or even touched. They must be felt with the heart. Helen Keller

✻ Think and wonder, wonder and think... Dr. Seuss

✻ Go confidently in the direction of your dreams. Live the life you've imagined. Thoreau

for the **road** *ahead*

Supplies: Patterned papers (Chatterbox); epoxy stickers (Creative Imaginations); quotes (www.dailycelebrations.com, Quote, Unquote/Autumn Leaves); mini brads (Boxer Scrapbook Productions); paper flowers (Making Memories); transparencies (Grafix); vellum

Random Advice...

Joanna designed the text for this insightful page with her epoxy stickers in mind. She first enlarged the font size of the select words the stickers would eventually replace. Joanna then printed drafts until she was confident the text was structured adequately to accommodate the stickers before deleting the enlarged words and printing onto a transparency. Vellum was adhered between the transparency and patterned paper to soften the look of the pattern before adhering the transparency to the page. Finally, the epoxy stickers were placed in their designated sentences.

Photo: Heather Preckle, Swannanoa, North Carolina

TIP: In order to make clear epoxy word stickers more legible against patterned paper, first affix the stickers to white cardstock, then trim away the excess before mounting over a background.

Sweet Childish Days

By layering a printed transparency over a single large photo, Joanna strategically made use of sentiments perfectly suited to her page theme. Large sheets of mica sandwiched between layers of patterned papers and secured with adhesive provide a subtle border for the top and bottom of the layout.

Photo: FoxFish Photography, Arvada, Colorado

TRICK: Experiment with enlarging your photos and strategically layering them with printed transparencies, making sure to position the preprinted designs and text so that they work with the photo, cropping the overlay if necessary.

Sweet childish days, that were as long as twenty days are now. William Wordsworth

simple things of life
- Laura Ingalls Wilder

I can hardly wait 'til nighttime falls
When I climb into bed with my

Though she be but little, she be fierce. - Shakespeare

While Cheryl was out here on her trip to witness Chiara's birth, she mentioned that she would really like a photo of herself and the girls before she left. Unfortunately time got away from us and the end of her trip was here before we knew it, so the morning of her departure I threw together my garage "studio", grabbed my mother-in-law and the girls, and started shooting away. Anna had NO interest whatsoever in sitting still, taking direction, or listening to me in general, so the shoot was kind of a circus with both Cheryl and I using every trick we could think of to lure Anna back to where I had set things up. When I got the prints back, I was pleasantly surprised by how many wonderful shots I managed to get in spite of Anna's efforts to be contrary, and this one is probably my favourite. I love how it reflects the overwhelming love of a grandmother for her only grandchildren, the closeness of a family full of people that are demonstratively loving with each other, the beauty of two generations of Pesce girls, and the preciousness of new life. 6.11.04

Supplies: Patterned papers (Chatterbox); printed transparency (Memories Complete); molding (Making Memories) circle accent (EK Success); peach paper dye (7 Gypsies); mica; pink cardstock

Giggle

It can be tricky to determine how to use patterned paper and preprinted transparencies. Here Joanna expertly combined the two to create an appealing layout. A play-themed, definition-style printed transparency layered over aged-paint patterned paper creates a unique look and provides instant custom journaling.

Photos: Mark Bolick, Fletcher, North Carolina

TRICK: Layering patterned paper with preprinted transparencies offers a quick and easy way to add depth, visual variety and balance to a layout.

Supplies: Textured red cardstock (Bazzill); patterned paper (Karen Foster Design); canvas phrase, flower, number stickers (Li'l Davis Designs); spiral clip, transparency (7 Gypsies); playing card bookmark (EK Success); rub-ons (Making Memories); ribbon; brown ink

At the Beach

A collage of clear elements makes for an eye-appealing addition to this seaside page. Joanna began by stamping on mica with black Staz On ink. She then used Diamond Glaze to attach the mica to three cropped bookmarks. Next, Joanna layered the assemblage with cut elements from printed transparencies, attaching them using two decorative clips and Diamond Glaze.

TRICK: Utilize fun accents such as decorative clips to help hold your clear elements in place. Joanna also recommends Diamond Glaze, which produces a glossy finish, for adhering mica and transparencies to paper. Clear-drying glue and vellum tape can also be used with transparent elements.

Supplies: Textured brown cardstock (Bazzill); patterned paper, bookmarks, clip, stamp (EK Success); rub-ons, vacation definition, washer, paper tags, flower brad (Making Memories); black clip and patterned paper (7 Gypsies); stickers (Pebbles); printed transparency (Memories Complete); stencil, index tabs, file folder (Autumn Leaves); diamond glaze (JudiKins); ribbon (K & Company); mica (USArtQuest); solvent ink (Tsukineko); vellum; sandpaper

TRICK: To make the snowflake images appear aged as opposed to bright white, Joanna simply turned the mica pieces over before adhering them to the page.

Supplies: Patterned paper, leather accent (Rusty Pickle); mica (USArtQuest); snowflake stamp (PSX Design); watermark ink (Tsukineko); mini rub-on (Making Memories); brown ink; walnut ink; white embossing powder; ribbon; eyelets

WHAT COULD BE BETTER THAN A SNOW DAY? THANKS TO A FEBRUARY SNOWSTORM, JOSH HAD THE OPPORTUNITY TO ENJOY THIS WINTERY DAY FOR ALL IT WAS WORTH. CONVINCING HIM TO COME BACK INSIDE THE HOUSE WAS THE HARDEST PART! 2.26.04

CHERISH
the *little* moments

Cherish the Little Moments

For their glassy appearance and tactile dimension, Joanna's embossed mica elements almost appear to be sheets of ice resting on the fence post that frames this young outdoor enthusiast's face. By stamping onto mica with embossing ink and embossing with white embossing powder, Joanna achieved a wonderful wintry effect perfect for a snow-day page.

Photo: Judith Fender, Fletcher, North Carolina

Stamp image of snowflake onto mica with embossing ink.

Sprinkle with white embossing powder; tap off excess.

Heat emboss image.

Toddlerhood

A small section of mica placed over a cropped image of Joanna's son's face created an artistic framing effect. The uneven edges and askew placement helped to complement the rugged boyishness theme of a little guy coming into his own.

Supplies: Textured navy blue, red and taupe cardstocks (Bazzill); metal-rimmed tag (Making Memories); mica (USArtQuest); blue cardstock

TRICK: Layering small sections of mica over photo elements is an understated but effective way to draw additional focus.

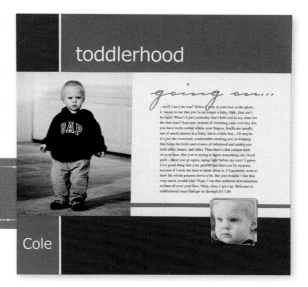

Sweet Childish Days

Although the semicircle journaling element appears to be vellum, it is actually a photo enhancement Joanna created using image editing software. To feature the endearing expressions on the children's faces center-stage, Joanna enlarged the photo and created the faux vellum element to occupy the right side for a graphic touch.

Photo: Judith Fender, Fletcher, North Carolina

Supplies: Patterned paper (Chatterbox); wooden flower (Li'l Davis Designs); photo editing software (Adobe Photoshop); black cardstock

TECHNIQUE: Create a partially transparent photo element in Adobe Photoshop by selecting the ellipse tool and drawing a circle on top of the photo. Select white for the circle's color then reduce its opacity to make it more transparent using the slider tool found on the layers panel. Position the circle to only partially overlap the photo.

The Tractor

To accentuate the earthy nature of her layout, Joanna created a mica page border inked in haphazard fashion using the tires of a toy car. The messy, muddy look of the miniature tracks works effectively to enhance the tractor theme, and was achieved by aligning the pieces in rows, running the car over the sheets and placing them along the top and side of the page.

Supplies: Text patterned paper, clip (7 Gypsies); red patterned paper (Paper Loft); rub-ons, stencil, index tab, file folder (Autumn Leaves); mica (USArtQuest); black acrylic paint; black cardstock;

TIP: For applying ink to mica, utilize a solvent based ink such as Tsukineko's Staz On for best results.

So Sick

Here printing on vellum created visual interest in combination with a bold, stamped title. To achieve the dimensional and glossy look of the letters, Joanna first applied white acrylic paint to foam letter stamps and stamped partially over the photo and vellum. Once dry, she stamped over the letters with black acrylic paint. After the second application was dry, Joanna applied Diamond Glaze to each letter for sheen.

Supplies: Textured black and white cardstocks (Bazzill); textured blue paper (source unknown); patterned vellum (KI Memories); alphabet stamps (Making Memories); diamond glaze (JudiKins); black and white acrylic paints

TRICK: To print on vellum, Joanna selected the transparency setting on her computer and used a heat gun to set the wet ink.

Embrace

Three different clear elements combine to make an artful impression on this page. Joanna printed her journaling on a transparency that was then layered over patterned paper. To dress up and add emphasis to her smaller photo, Joanna applied a clear definition sticker directly over it and trimmed it to size. She then slipped the photo into a clear product packaging envelope, applied rub-on words and mounted it to the layout.

TIP: Make creative use of product packaging for instant and innovative page additions perfect for housing photos, journaling and embellishments.

Supplies: Textured black and brown cardstocks (Bazzill); patterned papers (MOD, my own design); bookplate, canvas word (Creative Imaginations); clear definition sticker, rub-on words (Making Memories); transparency (Grafix); clear plastic product packaging

Window Seat

By using two 8½ x 11" transparencies that she printed herself, Joanna more economically achieved the look of a single 12 x 12" pre-printed sheet. The size, placement and color of the text were adjusted to correspond with her photo. Each sheet was then trimmed and layered horizontally over the enlarged photo for depth. Empty red frames form a unique page border and strategically reinforce the window and clear page element themes.

TECHNIQUE: Joanna created her text using Adobe InDesign, but the same look can be created in word processing programs such as Microsoft Word.

Supplies: Patterned paper (Sweetwater); red frames (Li'l Davis Designs); page layout software (Adobe InDesign); transparencies

WIN-DOW SEAT

4.04

The house is quiet - toooo quiet. I warily peek into Cole's room, wondering what new discovery my darling child has made now. Past experience has taught me to expect a tube of desitin smeared across his face and hands, or the contents of the diaper pail strewn across the room... BUT WAIT, what is this? My mobile toddler is sitting quietly at the window, completely absorbed in the scene across the street. As I silently rejoice for the hubbub of a concrete truck I had previously classified as "annoying," I grab my camera and document this moment of peace. Then I kneel down and join Cole at the window, ready to share in the thrill of a room with a view.

Supplies: Patterned paper, file folder, letter stamps (Rusty Pickle); word patterned paper, mini tags (Making Memories); Mickey Mouse patterned paper (Sandylion); clip (7 Gypsies); clear overlay (Memories Complete); black cardstock; transparency; blue gingham and brown ribbons; black ink

It's The Simple Things

Taking a cue from her son's endearing captivation with his toy car, Joanna was inspired to chronicle more of the "simple things" he so enjoys—including dirt, dogs and remote controls. Joanna cut apart a printed transparency and used one element for her title, which was casually stapled to the file folder accent. Journaling printed onto a transparency and accompanying photos are housed inside.

TRICK: When printing on transparencies, print on the rough surface side. If you like the glossy appearance, simply select the "reverse text" or "flip horizontal" option on your printer setting before printing. Be sure to choose the correct type of transparency for your printer.

2003

What a blast this summer ha[...]
with you at Waldenburg Par[...]
usually head to the p[...]
naptime...all recharged and [...]
think your favorite part is c[...]
stairs to the slide. In fact, [...]
reason you actually slide d[...]
right back up again. I love yo[...]
this picture...it certainl[...]
much fun playin[...]

PARK

play

Jennifer BOURGEAULT

GEOMETRIC SHAPES

In the summer of 2001 as her son's first birthday approached, Jennifer noticed the photos documenting his first year beginning to pile up. Following the advice of friends, she began perusing local scrapbook stores seeking creative ways to chronicle her mounting collection. Before long, Jennifer discovered the online scrapbooking community, at which point she says her self-described "obsession" with the craft began.

Unsure of just how her signature style of using bold geometric shapes developed, Jennifer imagines it was shortly after she discovered the benefits of the circle cutter, a tool that quickly became a much-used favorite. According to Jennifer, "Ever since I started this hobby, I have always preferred clean lines on my scrapbook pages. I don't think I have ever tilted a picture on any of my pages! Even my home is very clutter-free and decorated with clean lines." Utilizing shapes and crisp lines allows Jennifer to artfully incorporate her photos and the stories behind them into her overall layout design, an aspect of the craft she considers to be her strength. "Using geometric shapes such as circles and squares makes it easier for me to follow the principles of design." As for how to best work striking shapes and linear elements into a design, Jennifer suggests "cutting strips and circles from different papers and moving them around until they look just right."

When not planning her next creation, Jennifer teaches classes at her local scrapbook store and is a wife to Jason and stay-at-home mom to Connor and Lillian. She resides in Macomb Township, Michigan.

...Little Face

Jennifer worked her circle cutter to come up with an appealing layout boasting several of her signature shapes. Visual interest was easily added by applying square and rectangle letter stickers to circles cut from patterned paper and foam adhesive-popped metal-rimmed tags. Crisp border strips lend a linear element to the layout while a triangle provides visual weight to the bottom right corner.

TRICK: Jennifer cut a premade frame to form her oversized page corner, which was sanded to create a muted, aged effect.

THAT ADORABLE

little FACE

Connor ~ Whether serious or smiling, silly or goofy... you have the most adorable little face I have ever seen!

April 2004

Supplies: Textured blue cardstock (Bazzill); patterned papers, premade frame, letter stickers (Daisy D's); letter stickers (Paper Loft); metal-rimmed tags (Making Memories); circle cutter (Provo Craft)

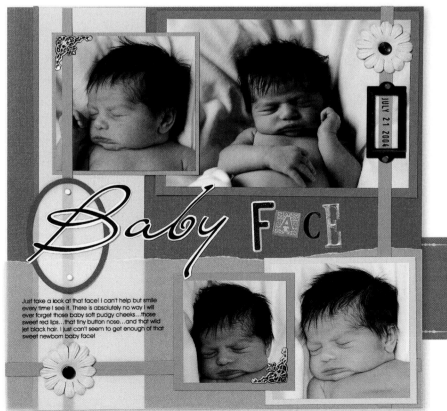

JULY 21 2004

Baby Face

Just take a look at that face! I can't help but smile every time I see it. There is absolutely no way I will ever forget those baby soft pudgy cheeks...those sweet red lips...that tiny button nose...and that wild jet block hair. I just can't seem to get enough of that sweet newborn baby face!

Baby Face

To feature her newborn daughter's darling frame-worthy face, Jennifer chose bold and colorful square photo mats. Overlapping the photos creates visual depth while cardstock strips run the length and width of the page. An oval metal-rimmed tag, label holder and square letter sticker lend additional shapes for good measure.

TECHNIQUE: Layering is an especially eye-catching technique to employ when working with shapes for the instant dimension it adds to the page.

Supplies: Textured red, yellow, purple, green and blue card-stocks (Bazzill); paper flowers, date stamp (Making Memories); metal label holder (Magic Scraps); metal photo corners (source unknown); oval metal-rimmed tag (Colorbök); letter stickers (Creative Imaginations, Me & My Big Ideas, Sticker Studio); black buttons, vellum, brads

...*Ballgame*

Playing off her ballgame theme, Jennifer mimicked the look of actual baseballs with a bold circle photo frame, title element and hand-stitched journaling block. Red cardstock strips and circle letter stickers continue the graphic, geometric-inspired design while cropped photo blocks and a diamond mesh sticker pull in additional shapes.

TIP: Look for such creative finishing touches as Jennifer's hand-stitched elements to put your own layouts over the top.

Supplies: *Green patterned paper (Mustard Moon); textured red cardstock (Bazzill); round letter stickers (Memories Complete); large letter stickers (Sticker Studio); black acrylic stickers (KI Memories); wooden letter stickers (Li'l Davis Designs); diamond mesh sticker (Tumblebeasts); date rub-ons (Autumn Leaves); circle cutter (Provo Craft); embroidery floss; white cardstock*

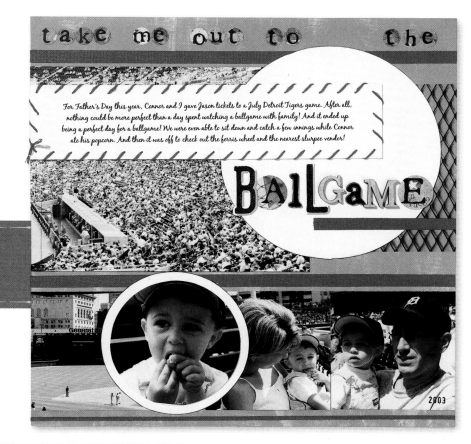

For Father's Day this year, Connor and I gave Jason tickets to a July Detroit Tigers game. After all, nothing could be more perfect than a day spent watching a ballgame with family! And it ended up being a perfect day for a ballgame! We were even able to sit down and catch a few innings while Connor ate his popcorn. And then it was off to check out the ferris wheel and the nearest slurpee vendor!

Slush

A slushee cup gave Jennifer all the inspiration she needed to design the details of this sweet summertime layout. Textured cardstock was dry brushed with red acrylic paint to bring out its square pattern and mimic the cup design. Color blocking, various strips of cardstock and mesh add bold, graphic layers while a cardstock circle echoes the slushee's domed lid.

Nothing beats an ice cold slush on a hot summer day! And Connor loves his slushes! In fact, we can't go anywhere these days without stopping for one. Red is his absolute favorite, with blue coming in a close second. And Mommy loves how happy an ice cold slush can make her little boy!

TIP: In addition to simply incorporating colors from photos, pull artistic details from one or more elements to carry over into your design choices.

Supplies: *Textured cardstock (source unknown); textured black and blue cardstocks (Bazzill); label holder (Li'l Davis Designs); mesh (Magic Mesh); circle template (Provo Craft); white, black and blue papers; red acrylic paint*

...Motherhood

Here an attractive floral-patterned paper circle proves frames needn't always be square or rectangular in shape. Jennifer used a circle cutter to form the shape, then cut out the center to create visual impact and add focus to her journaling and photo. The grid-like mesh, photo mat and bold cardstock section spanning the page add square and rectangle shapes, while an additional circle and sanded pattern paper strips complete the design.

TRICK: As a fun and understated design detail, Jennifer used a circle-shaped brad as a punctuation mark at the end of her title quote.

Supplies: Patterned paper (Making Memories); mesh (Magic Mesh); bookplate (source unknown); decorative trim (Me & My Big Ideas); circle cutter (Provo Craft); transparency; brad

Within the circle photo: *Becoming your mother has become the best and most beautiful thing that has ever happened in my life. Because of you, I have found happiness inside me that I never even knew existed. Thank you, sweet Connor.*

Oh the power of motherhood.

Connor & Mama July 2003

Happy New Year, Baby!

Many shapes make their way onto this playful party-themed page. Cardstock border strips are embellished with metal-rimmed tags layered with a small circle, mesh and star-adorned party hats. Patterned paper and a double-matted title treatment bring in additional circle shapes, while various-sized cropped photos lend straight lines to the layout.

TIP: Take cues from fun patterned papers to repeat design elements and color schemes for an eye-pleasing page.

Connor, Devon and Jemma getting an early start on the 2004 New Year celebration!

Supplies: Patterned paper (SEI); textured green, light green, blue and brown cardstocks (Bazzill); metal-rimmed tags (Making Memories); party hats, "happy" embellishment (EK Success); mesh (Magic Mesh); circle template (Provo Craft); vellum

Priceless

Circle punches were used to custom-create a whimsical pattern along the top of this page. A premade frame accent layered over a journaling block and enlarged, cropped photo incorporate striking square shapes. For a crisp means of keeping her design contained, Jennifer adds cardstock borders for linear elements.

TRICK: By utilizing a frame accent, Jennifer easily and artfully distinguished her personal journaling from the page title and accompanying quote.

Supplies: Textured green and light green cardstocks (Bazzill); frame (My Mind's Eye); label holder (Making Memories); circle punch (Creative Memories); copper brads; brown and slate cardstocks

You are such a priceless gift! I may never get that home on the lake or that new diamond ring, but being able to see you every waking moment is so much more valuable than anything I have had to forgo. I believe that my decision to stay at home and raise you has become the most rewarding experience of my life. Thank you so much, sweet Connor, and I look forward to many more priceless moments with you!

You are the trip I did not take,
You are the pearls I cannot buy,
You are my blue Italian lake,
YOU ARE MY PIECE OF FOREIGN SKY.

May 2003

Bath Time

Paper and vellum circles that mimic bath-time bubbles and crisp, linear borders help create the clean look of this layout. Jennifer formed her eye-catching oval title element by rounding the corners of a large rectangle to showcase handcut letters. A circle cutter and circle punch were used to create the square mesh-matted circle border and bubbles. A bath towel embellishment introduces yet another circle element into the layout.

PuRe   clEaN   FrESh

If it's bath time, Connor can certainly be found with a smile on his face. He absolutely loves splishing and splashing around in a bubble filled bathtub! And getting to take a bath in the big hot tub makes it all the better. These pictures were taken during one of many bath times in January 2004.

TIP: Incorporate a basic shape into a layout in an entirely unique way as Jennifer did here by making it span the length of the page.

Supplies: Textured green and light blue cardstocks (Bazzill); bath towel accent (EK Success); mesh (Magic Mesh); letter stickers (Chatterbox); white and blue cardstocks; corner rounder; vellum

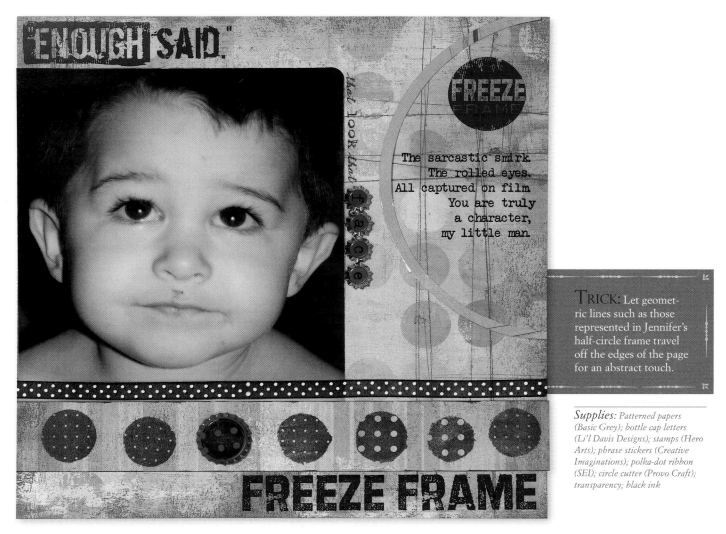

"ENOUGH SAID."

that look that face

FREEZE FRAME

The sarcastic smirk.
The rolled eyes.
All captured on film
You are truly
a character,
my little man.

FREEZE FRAME

Supplies: Patterned papers (Basic Grey); bottle cap letters (Li'l Davis Designs); stamps (Hero Arts); phrase stickers (Creative Imaginations); polka-dot ribbon (SEI); circle cutter (Provo Craft); transparency; black ink

Enough Said

Seeing spots takes on all-new meaning in this fun and eye-appealing page. Circle and striped patterned papers helped to provide inspiration for Jennifer's choices of adding polka-dot ribbon and whimsical bottle cap elements. For a stylish twist, a half circle frames transparency-printed journaling.

Punch small circle from scrap paper for template.

Cut 1½" strip from the striped patterned paper. Place circle template over striped paper and stamp directly onto your template. This will change the square stamp image into a circle shape on the paper.

Move template over and repeat second step along entire strip, changing stamp as desired.

Birthday Wishes

One look at the fun colors and shapes in these geometric-patterned papers and Jennifer knew they would be the perfect inspiration for this birthday page. Multi-colored buttons layered with letter stickers placed over the circle pattern provide a unique title treatment. A strip of molding, die-cut-adorned circle frames and metal-rimmed tags layered with coordinating papers and buttons continue the circle theme. A strategically chosen font showcases the word "wish," which was woven throughout the journaling passage.

Supplies: Patterned paper, circle frames, letter stickers, molding (Chatterbox); candle die cuts (Sizzix); metal-rimmed tags (Making Memories); buttons (Junkitz)

TIP: Shapes needn't always be limited to "extra" embellishments. When working bold shapes and lines into your layouts, look to patterned papers to help determine the colors and direction of your design.

Donuts

Jennifer had no trouble incorporating her signature shapes into this layout featuring her son enjoying a donut. Several details contribute to the cohesiveness of the circle-inspired design, including embossed paper, circle frames and a circle journaling element. These accents, as well as the title, were treated with various stamping inks to resemble donuts. Additionally, Jennifer hand sewed buttons like those on her son's shirt onto the bold rectangle mat.

Supplies: Textured paper (source unknown); textured green cardstock (Bazzill); circle frames (Chatterbox); label holder, twine (Magic Scraps); buttons (Junkitz); circle template (Provo Craft); brown, cream and beige cardstocks; plum embroidery floss; brads; various brown stamping inks

TIP: Look to small accents such as hand-sewn buttons, colored brads and rectangle label holders to add easy, instant geometric elements to your pages.

Spring Training

Having captured the sequence of this future hall-of-famer's first hitting attempts, Jennifer featured each individual action shot with square-cropped photos and photo mats. Additional squares are echoed throughout the design using epoxy stickers, and even block-style journaling printed on the textured cardstock background is in keeping with her square-inspired page design. Bright, primary-colored cardstock strips keep the lines of the composition clean and linear.

Supplies: Textured cardstock (Bazzill); baseball stickers (S.R.M. Press); epoxy stickers (Creative Imaginations); date rub-on (Autumn Leaves)

TRICK: In addition to adding artistic flair, square-cropping eliminates visual distractions and makes featuring several photos on a single page easier.

Brand New

Striped and polka-dot-patterned papers provide striking visual interest in this layout dedicated to the arrival of Jennifer's baby daughter. A bold circle background element is inked and layered with several coordinating patterned paper rectangles, which echo the shape of the enlarged photo. Square and rectangle cardboard letters and dome epoxy letter stickers add dimension, while a circle metal-rimmed tag featuring a punched paper element round out the page design.

TRICK: By simply using a corner rounder on her rectangle border accents, Jennifer quickly and easily softened the look of the bold shapes.

Supplies: Patterned papers, book cloth phrase (Chatterbox); metal-rimmed tag (Making Memories); epoxy dome stickers (K & Company); cardboard letters (Li'l Davis Designs); circle punch (Creative Memories); circle cutter (Provo Craft)

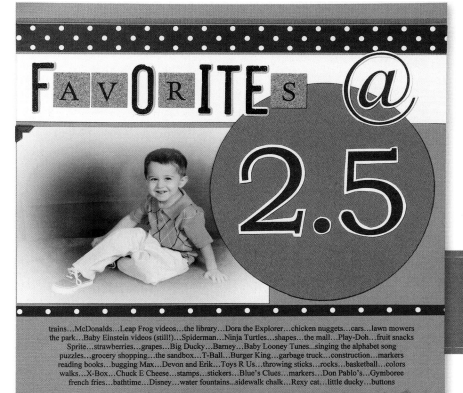

Favorites @ 2.5

Clad in an argyle shirt and converse-style shoes, this 1950s-esque black-and-white photo of Jennifer's son inspired her to try out her signature style with a bit of a retro feel. Polka-dot patterned paper strips were incorporated for graphic borders. A large circle and numerous punched circles create crisp geometric accents and add a striking splash of color. Title treatment details such as the circular "at" symbol and select square cork letters introduce additional shapes into the design for good measure.

TIP: Try combining multiple geometric shapes to add visual interest to a design otherwise dominated by purely rounded or angular lines.

Supplies: Textured cardstock (Bazzill); patterned paper (Chatterbox); letter stickers (Sticker Studio); cork letter stickers (Artistic Scrapper); circle cutter (Provo Craft); circle punch (Marvy); black ink

The Mickey Pool

Inspired by the design of the Mickey Mouse pool her son so enjoyed during a Disney cruise, Jennifer found a fun way to include oversized circles to showcase journaling and a photo. A crisp photo mat and thin cardstock strips comprise other signature elements of this graphic composition.

TECHNIQUE: To create stand-out circle frame accents, use a circle cutter and consider cropping portions of the elements for visual interest.

Supplies: Textured black, green, red and yellow cardstocks; letter stickers (Sticker Studio); dimensional letters (Creative Imaginations); patterned vellum (American Crafts); tag (Making Memories); Mickey Stamp (source unknown); circle cutter (Provo Craft); brads; white cardstock

The Patch

Jennifer conceived yet another creative use for circle accents in this endearing layout. In order to replicate the wagon wheels of the radio flyer featured in the photo, white cardstock was added to the backs of premade circle frames with silver brads set in their centers. These charming accents add the perfect touch to her title treatment, which also features an understated cardstock strip and inked square letter elements.

TIP: Shapes can be found everywhere. Look to your photos to find geometric elements that can easily be pulled out and mimicked in the form of page accents.

Supplies: Textured blue paper (source unknown); textured brown cardstock (Bazzill); vellum letter stickers (Mrs.. Grossman's); square letters (Foofala); pumpkin charm (source unknown); circle scrapbook frames (Chatterbox); walnut ink (Autumn Leaves); stamping ink

Susan CYRUS

Playful Page Themes

A friend led Susan to scrapbooking several years ago, but it wasn't until early 2003 that she settled into a style that suited her artistic tastes. Inspired by the antics of her husband and young son, Susan set out to creatively capture the slice-of-life moments and details of daily life that are often overlooked.

Susan attributes her whimsical signature style and use of playful page themes to purchasing a digital camera after the birth of her child. Once the expense of film developing wasn't a limitation, Susan began photographing a much wider range of subjects. "The more I paid attention to the 'little things' in life, the more I began to develop a preference for scrapbooking topics that are humorous, lighthearted or presented from an unusual perspective." To enhance the fun and casual feel of her layouts, Susan often employs the use of bright colors, humorous juxtapositions, plays on words, double-entendres, funky fonts, witty journaling and haphazard arrangement as creative strategies. While many scrapbookers categorize themselves as 'event' scrapbookers, Susan refers to herself as more of a 'moment' scrapbooker...but with a twist. "The 'moments' that I encounter are more likely to be something along the lines of my son drinking out of a dog dish or eating crayons than posing sweetly for a portrait or staring peacefully out the window. We're quirky. We're imperfect. I just try to pay attention to the details and run with it."

In addition to her scrapbooking, Susan works as a feature page designer for a newspaper. She lives in Broken Arrow, Oklahoma, with husband Alvin and son Connor.

Running With the Bulls

Strategic paper and product choices enhance the rugged theme and humorous title of this layout. Susan used a font in Adobe Photoshop to create "mud splatters," while lighthearted photos and playful hidden journaling lend additional humor to the design and page theme.

Primary photo: Renee Coffey, Edgewater, Colorado

TRICK: To keep her embellishments from competing with her photos, Susan steered clear of silly and opted for stripes, solids, and subtle prints.

Supplies: Patterned papers (Chatterbox, Karen Foster Design, Paper Loft); metal-rimmed tag (Making Memories); image editing software (Adobe Photoshop); green and cream cardstocks; raffia; pen

Duck... Duck... Goose!

Susan's son's chase-and-throw approach to feeding the ducks inspired her to create an off-kilter composition with fun and quirky design choices. Here her page theme plays off the children's game Duck Duck Goose, which aptly described Connor's silly strategy, rendering him a "silly goose." Susan's atypical placement of her software-generated title, page embellishments and humorous journaling contribute to the sense of whimsy.

TIP: Experiment with taking photos from different angles for a playful perspective, such as from behind your subject as Susan did here in her focal photo. Moreover, intentionally place page elements at askew angles for a subtle way of emphasizing a silly situation or a person's unusual behavior.

Supplies: Patterned paper (Design Originals); mica (USArtQuest); slide mounts (Designer's Library); image editing software (Adobe Photoshop); vellum; pen; ribbon

...Goosed

Assuming her son would be enthralled with the animal whose name had become a favorite vocabulary word, Susan was surprised by the indifference he displayed during an introductory encounter at the park...and the absence of the word "duck" in his speech ever since. Hence, a dual opportunity to play off the word "goose" presented itself. Susan effectively contradicted the scene represented in her focal photo with witty journaling, highlighting the word "duck" with acrylic pebbles. In combination with the bold presentation of the word "goosed," Susan plays off both the children's game and the feeling that she had been duped.

TIP: Keep in mind book titles, nursery rhymes, catch phrases, song lyrics and the like for fun inclusions in your titles and journaling.

We took Connor to feed ducks for the first time last weekend. "Duck" has been one of his favorite words lately: he giggles and says it over and over ... "Duck. Duck. Duck." But to my surprise, he was not exactly enthralled with those ducks. He preferred running up and down the hill. In fact he hasn't said the word "duck" since we brought him home.

I guess Alvin and I got **goosed**.

March 2004
26 months

Supplies: Patterned vellum (Design Originals); acrylic pebbles (Making Memories); photo corners (Canson); blue vellum; transparency; red paper

Uncle Chad,

Aunt Carol, and the object of your affection, your 'canine cousin,' Chance.

CONNOR

remember

remember

OCT 03
21 mos

You are not a DOG

MAY 04
2¼ yrs

Even though you crawled into Chance's cage and refused to come out, you are not a dog.

Even though you can bark and pant like a champ, you are not a dog.

Even though I caught you on all-fours at Aunt Carol's 30th birthday party, licking water out of Chance's dish and declaring, 'Mmmmm!,' you are not a dog.

So don't even think about drinking out of the toilet, ok?

You Are Not a Dog

Susan humorously captured her son's preoccupation with all things canine in this playful page. Silly candid photos and journaling effectively contradict one another to create a mixed message while a messy typewriter font and walnut-ink-stained patterned paper add to the fun feel. A clever "punch-line" is printed along the bottom edge of the page and is highlighted with mica tiles for emphasis.

TECHNIQUE: Repeat key portions of your journaling and change its size or color to create an instant sense of playfulness and additional impact.

Supplies: Patterned paper (Design Originals); labels (Dymo); mica (USArtQuest); stamp (All Night Media); ribbon, brad, metal-rimmed tag (Making Memories); pen; ink; embossing powder

Supplies: Stained-glass paint (Krylon); solvent ink (Tsukineko); letter stamps (All Night Media); white cardstock; string; transparency; fabric scraps; pen

We hadn't allowed him TOMATO sauce in a year.

I thought he might be too picky to even try it.

I shouldn't have worried.

He took one look at that plate of spaghetti and dived in with GUSTO He SLURPED. He stuffed.

And by the time he was done, he looked like a little CLOWN with his sauce-stained cheeks.

He didn't even notice the meat in the sauce! Now that was a red-letter day!

Seeing Red

Susan devised a creative page background to commemorate the successful introduction of spaghetti into her son's finicky diet. By assembling string on transparencies and spraying them with stained-glass paint, a striking resemblance to saucy noodles was achieved. Photos of Susan's son with his fists full endearingly counter the concept of "seeing red," a title that holds dual meaning for the meal's messy outcome. A ribbon and string border and multifont journaling make for playful page additions.

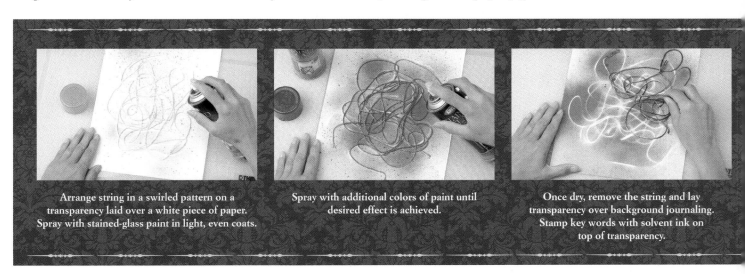

Arrange string in a swirled pattern on a transparency laid over a white piece of paper. Spray with stained-glass paint in light, even coats.

Spray with additional colors of paint until desired effect is achieved.

Once dry, remove the string and lay transparency over background journaling. Stamp key words with solvent ink on top of transparency.

PB Wars

Once Susan saw the photos that resulted from a father-son lunchtime standoff, the idea for a layout of "opposing forces" fell instantly into place. Though her photos share obvious similarities, the contrast of the black and white backgrounds conjured images of "good versus evil" when cleverly paired side by side. Susan added "sticky fingerprints" of both her husband and son for a fun touch as well as an extreme close-up of the rejected food at issue to create a page requiring little editorializing.

Supplies: Patterned Paper (Karen Foster Design); tag (2Dye4); labels (Dymo); date stamp (Making Memories); letter stamps (Fontwerks, Hero Arts); orange, white and black cardstocks; ink; acrylic paint; photo corner

TIP: Randomly combine upper- and lowercase alphabet stamps of varying fonts for playful and casual journaling and titles.

What Did You Expect?

Here Susan cleverly played off of the popular pregnancy manual "What to Expect When You're Expecting" with a silly photo featuring three pregnant bellies. A journaling passage dramatically detailing the waiting process sets the stage for the humorous photo, which is allowed to shine with understated page accents and a computer-generated page background.

Photo: Joan Fox, Lafayette, California

Supplies: Negative strip (Creative Imaginations); ribbon (Making Memories); image editing software (Adobe Photoshop)

TECHNIQUE: Create your own page backgrounds by using a font to create a line drawing using software such as Adobe Photoshop for a custom-created background.

He's Got a Ticket to Ride...

Susan called upon a classic song title by juxtaposing photos of her son's emotional extremes during a trip to an amusement part. Bright colors, whimsical patterned papers, paint and polar-opposite photos make for a humorous composition. Far from being a "wasted" moment, the meltdown captured in the secondary photo provides a comical touch and endearing contrast to the layout.

Supplies: Patterned paper (Karen Foster Design); acrylic paint (Plaid); white cardstock; pen; ink

TECHNIQUE: Susan employed her camera's slow synchronized flash function to create her striking focal photo, which utilizes a flash to freeze action in the foreground and to cast otherwise uninteresting backgrounds into dynamic blurs and streaks.

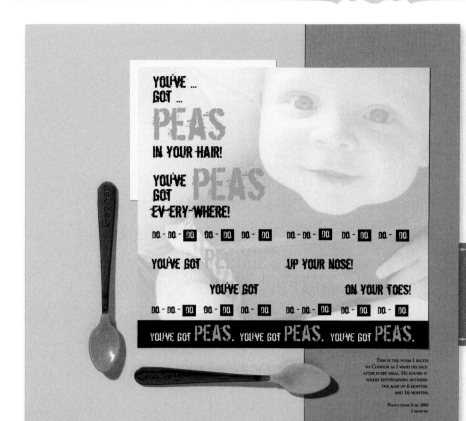

You've Got Peas...

A wacky and playful typographical treatment was used to feature a poem Susan recites to her son after each messy mealtime. Colorful baby spoons make for fun page additions and a simple yet bold cardstock background keeps the emphasis on the screened photo and manipulated text.

TECHNIQUE: Susan added text to a screened photo using Adobe Photoshop, changing the size and color of key words for emphasis.

Supplies: Baby spoons (Gerber); textured green cardstock (Bazzill); image editing software (Adobe Photoshop); orange cardstock

Sprinkled

An afternoon romp in the sprinkler is illustrated with whimsical stitched swirls and randomly scattered jewel accents. Torn patterned paper with rolled edges adds a fun splash of color to contrast the white background. The casual typeface used in the title perfectly complements the feel of the page, while imprecise border stitching reflects a sense of spontaneity and playfulness.

TECHNIQUE: To create her stitched swirls, Susan first used a pencil to lightly draw the shape onto cardstock. She then machine stitched along the lines, adding the jewel baubles and erasing any visible pencil marks.

Supplies: Patterned papers (Bo-Bunny Press, Creative Imaginations); jewels (Me & My Big Ideas, Westrim); white cardstock; pen; thread

Ode to My Honda

Rather than describing a car accident in just-the-facts fashion, Susan used melodramatic journaling to chronicle the event. A letter directed to her newly departed vehicle made for a unique and lighthearted approach for detailing a frustrating event. A filigree photo corner gives the photo of the smiley face air freshener an exaggerated importance while the simple and graphic design treatment keeps the focus on the story.

TIP: Get playful with the perspective from which you record events and tell stories to offer a fresh take on a situation.

Supplies: Brads and washer words (Making Memories); filigree photo corner (Boutique Trims); image editing software (Adobe Photoshop); white cardstock; aluminum sheet

Ode to my Honda

oh '93 Civic, things just haven't been the same since you've been gone. I've missed you so.

You were just a baby when we parted ways in February. Eleven years old, with only 100,000 miles on your odometer. You still had a lot of living left to do.

when that unlicensed, uninsured motorist took you from me in the intersection of 51st St. and Hwy 169, you never saw it coming. You put up a brave fight, but alas, the blow was too much for your small frame, and you were declared a total loss, sigh ...

I have tried to carry on in Alvin's old Prizm.

but it feels so strange to be away from you. We welcomed a new Blazer into the garage the day after your accident, and now the whole garage dynamic has changed.

You served me well for the nine years we were together. May you rest in peace. May 2004

WATCH

you said as you lead me to the VCR. "This one." Your chubby hands pushed a neon green tape into mine. "Sit," you instructed. A week later it was, "Sit down."

These are just a few of the words you have begun to say lately, and they all have one thing in common. Veggie Tales.

I had purchased a Veggie Tales video at a consignment store in April. I was familiar with the concept (cartoon vegetables tell Bible stories) and with the characters, Bob the Tomato and Larry the Cucumber, but I had never actually seen the show. You had been reluctant to accept much TV other than Sesame Street, which you adored.

I popped it in to see your reaction. That was all it took. You were officially addicted to Veggies. Two months later, we own two more Veggie Tales videos, have another eight on the way, and you balk at watching anything else.

"Veggies?" you ask from the moment you get up until the moment you go to bed. "Watch!" I feel funny saying this, but I think we are actually going to have to restrict the amount of Veggies in your diet.

"Songs!" you shout when the "Silly Songs with Larry" portion of the show comes on. You dance to all of it, but you put on a particularly impressive performance during the opening credits. First you run to the kitchen, where you rock back and forth from one leg to another. When Bob says, "Have we got a show for you," that is your cue to quickly hop onto the couch and bounce on your knees from one end of the couch to the other for the remainder of the song. Your choreography cracks us up!

Here are a few of the other words you've picked up from your daily dose of Veggies.

June 2004

Gotta Be Veggie Tales

Here Susan devised a clever way to showcase her son's obsession with "Veggie Tales" educational videos and the role the show has played in expanding his vocabulary. Actual scrabble tiles are used to highlight key words and are mounted to the page in actual game-playing formation. Striking colors, witty journaling and gleeful photo of the young fan make this page particularly fun.

TIP: Play up page themes with just-the-right fun and quirky product for instant impact.

Supplies: Scrabble game pieces (Hasbro); labels (Dymo); white, fluorescent green and fuchsia cardstocks

See spot.

roseola
July 2002 / 6 months

See spot play.

You were feeling pretty crummy just a few days before this, but you sure wouldn't know it from looking at these pictures! You were sent home from daycare with a fever of 104 and for a few days we weren't exactly sure what we were dealing with. by the time the rash appeared and we confirmed that this was roseola, the fever was gone and you were back to your happy self. with polkadots.

TRICK: When adding letter stamps to page elements, follow the lines of the shape as Susan did here with her punched circles for a fun variation.

Supplies: Letter stamps (All Night Media); spiral clips (Target); white, yellow and red cardstocks; acrylic paint; ink; pen; circle punch; bubble wrap

See Spot...

Although this layout chronicles a time when Susan's son was feeling under-the-weather, you'd never know it by his sunny demeanor and the cheerful, vibrant design of the page. Acrylic paint and bubble wrap combine to form a homemade stamp that, in addition to punched circles, plays off the rash young Connor developed during a bout of roseola. Susan cleverly called upon terminology from the iconic Dick and Jane book series in her title for the double meaning represented. Spiral clips, a smiley face and whimsically stamped words help keep the layout lighthearted.

Apply red paint over surface of large bubble wrap with fingers.

Press onto cardstock to create pattern. Allow to dry, then run through printer to add journaling.

At The Little Gym

To re-create the look and feel of a frenzied toddler gym class, Susan employed bold primary colors and fun page accents. Susan's multicolored text forms a page border and features strategically placed brads and labels for visual interest. Washers, acrylic baubles and a shoelace provide whimsical touches while sporadic journaling tidbits use a blend of fonts and stickers.

Supplies: Acrylic baubles (Making Memories); oversized brads (Hyglo); concho (Scrapworks); labels (Dymo); white cardstock; washers; shoelace; paint pen; pen

TECHNIQUE: Although her composition exudes fun and spontaneity, Susan maintained visual order through the use of a subtle background, repetition of accents and a hierarchy of sizes to keep individual elements from competing for attention.

Sesame Street Live

Bright colors, a clever title and fun typographical treatments combine to form this standout page. Susan's title is a takeoff of a sponsor tag line that appears during the broadcast of "Sesame Street." To make the title pop, "ransom" style lettering was incorporated and the text was cut into strips and assembled in free-form fashion. Text-patterned paper pulls in the very definition of "playful," while sparkling jewels create a border reminiscent of the stage lights shown in the photos.

Supplies: Patterned paper (7 Gypsies, Karen Foster Design); letter stickers (Pebbles); jewels (Me & My Big Ideas); foam alphabet stamps (Making Memories); black and white cardstocks

TIP: To keep several colorful photos from looking chaotic, try working with a simple black background.

Sweet

Endearing photos of Susan's son's enthusiasm for the spoils of Valentine's day are enhanced by his own "hand" crafted heart element. For additional playful touches, Susan included torn paper strips, a valentine from an admirer and journaling associated with the many connotations of the word "sweet" printed in two colors of ink. To add a little something extra to make the page pop, Susan bordered part of the heart element with knotted ribbon.

Supplies: Patterned paper (Wordsworth); bookplate (L'il Davis Designs); ribbon (Making Memories); white cardstock; brads; pen; valentine; child's art

TIP: Incorporating your child's artwork into a layout provides both instant whimsy and an engaging way to preserve his or her masterpieces.

Incredible.

In honor of Absolutely Incredible Kid Day, Susan expertly combined loving sentiment in a letter that at the same time details her son's precious quirks and silly characteristics. In order not to compete with the letter, Susan kept accents to a minimum, which include a patterned paper flower cut with a craft knife and various letter stickers to comprise a playful title treatment.

TIP: Susan's eye-catching title treatment was comprised entirely of "leftover" letter stickers. Scour your own stash of extra elements to see what fun and pleasing combinations you can come up with.

Supplies: Patterned paper (Karen Foster Design, KI Memories); sticker (Karen Foster Design); letter stickers (Creative Imaginations, K & Company, Memories Complete); button (Jesse James); white cardstock; pen

March 17, 2004

Dear Connor,

Tomorrow is Absolutely Incredible Kid Day, so I am writing to tell you that I think you're an absolutely incredible kid!

Who else but you could master a tricky puzzle the very first time you put it together?

Who else but you could eat three waffles for breakfast and still want some Cheerios for a snack?

Who else but you could wake me up so charmingly in the morning after Daddy gets you dressed for school?

Who else but you could keep the same face throughout the song, "If You're Happy and You Know It Clap Your Hands"? As your music teacher likes to say, whether we're singing about being happy, sad or angry, you're still HAPPY!!

Who else but you could spot a dessert or a meat product a mile away (the first to devour, the second to refuse)?

Who else but you could be my favorite boy in the whole wide world?

I love you Connor.

Love,

Mommy
xoxo

Two Baths On Easter

Rather than reporting the typical events of Easter, Susan celebrated her sticky-fingered son and the fact he required two trips to the bathtub for all the goodies he consumed. Painterly background paper and bunny paw print stamps help to heighten the holiday theme. Casually placed photos at off-kilter angles are surrounded by journaling strips detailing the array of food items eaten.

TIP: For those events that are similar from year to year, have fun with ways to recap the story and what unique highlights to include. In so doing the smaller details that are often overlooked can creatively be given center stage.

Supplies: Patterned papers (Karen Foster Design, Wordsworth); tag (2Dye4); paw stamp (All Night Media); letter stamps (Hero Arts); watermark ink (Tsukineko); blue and white cardstocks; mulberry; chalk; ribbon; transparencies; vellum

Susan

Here Susan turned the camera on herself to create a page packed with items that represent her life and personality. A favorite photo is flanked by an eclectic assortment of papers and page accents. Elements such as woven labels, mini file folders, rub-on letters and stickers all hold special significance, which at the same time make for an eye-appealing assemblage.

TECHNIQUE: Combine scraps, found items and premade embellishments to create a whimsical collage in a snap. By choosing elements that hold symbolic meaning, little editorializing is required which can help keep the page personal.

Supplies: Patterned paper (Design Originals, Pebbles, Scenic Route Paper Co.); woven labels, leather flowers, decorative brad, letter stamp, rub-on letters (Making Memories); ruler stickers, typewriter key sticker (EK Success); label holder (Magic Scraps); "simple pleasures" label (Me & My Big Ideas); mini file folders (Autumn Leaves); flower stickers (Paper House Productions); acrylic star (Westrim); heart charm (Scrapheap Re³); green and black cardstocks; buttons; ink; paint pen; playing card; scrabble tiles

Vacation in Hallsville

Silly photos of Susan's son and his oversized cap appear even more endearing with haphazard placement. This casual and fun look suggests the photos were tossed down and adhered where they happened to land. Adversely, strong horizontal and vertical lines and a string border add a sense of control to the design and allow for ample space alongside the focal photo. Susan's "recapping" of the events of her son's time with his grandparents also plays off of the focus of the hat.

TRICK: Make use of funny photos that may otherwise be deemed unworthy of scrapbooking with the help of journaling. Here Susan cleverly made use of photos of Connor's cap-disguised face with a humorous passage told from a fun angle.

Supplies: Patterned paper, woven label (Me & My Big Ideas); rivets (Chatterbox); labels (Dymo); cork (Magic Scraps); letter stamps (All Night Media, Hero Arts); photo corners; string; ink; acrylic paint

Sea

By the Beautiful Sea

SOME FORMS OF SHELLS

Jersey Girls

Mary

by the s

Mitre Shell

I love this photograph depicting the Jersey City McCarthy sisters with thei
New Jersey beach. I can almost hear them as they laugh and play together in
before being gathered together to have their picture taken. They look so sweet with th
bobbed-style haircuts and their ill-fitting swimsuits. And I must have looked at this photo a
times before I noticed the little dog peeking up from the sand at Mary's feet. Perhaps this cute lit
the source of Mary and Helen's distraction. He's the only one looking straight into the camera! Honey
be quite pleased with herself over her balancing act on Dad's back and the amused look on Rudy's face seem
that his girls are up to nothing more than their usual tricks.

Mary, Anna (Honey), Helen & John (Rudolf) McC

Lisa DIXON

JOURNALING

Lisa began scrapbooking in 1997, prior to the industry taking off in her home state of New Jersey. Having literally no scrapbooking stores to fuel her newfound interest, and armed only with her issue #2 of *Memory Makers* magazine, Lisa said she was forced for a time to teach herself the skills she saw represented in the pages and to order all of her supplies through the mail. Nearly eight years later, Lisa frequently sees her own layouts in our publications and teaches at one of several local scrapbook stores.

Having first explored scrapbooking as a means of displaying her photos, Lisa soon discovered the impracticality of constantly attempting to be "caught up" in capturing her family's everyday life in her albums. Resolving that it was both artistically freeing and acceptable to scrapbook non-chronologically, Lisa began to reconsider her creative motivation, which ultimately revealed her signature style. "That's when I began to listen to my voice and to realize that my voice and the stories I wanted to pass on are the real reasons I scrapbook. The pictures are wonderful but the stories behind them or inspired by them are just as wonderful." Now Lisa utilizes her love for words to create "illustrated life history" albums based not only on the events and occasions pictured, but also the emotions behind them. "The words are what give life to the pages—they make you laugh, they make you cry—sometimes both at once! And the versatility of words is amazing."

In addition to her scrapbook teaching and design work, Lisa is a full-time wife and mother to husband Fred and children Samantha and James in East Brunswick, New Jersey.

Nana's the Old Maid...Again!

To create a special page in honor of her grandmother, Lisa used an association technique to inspire her journaling passage. Fond childhood memories of playing the card game "Old Maid" prompted Lisa to build her page around vintage game cards she found on the Internet. The journaling revealed behind the hinged photo mat is printed on an enlarged "Old Maid" card image and details Lisa's recollections of her grandmother's knack for picking the infamous card.

TRICK: Use objects, smells, places and the like associated with special memories and people to creatively jump-start journaling and consequent page themes.

Supplies: Patterned paper (Memories Complete); lettering template (C-Thru Ruler); alphabet die cuts (QuicKutz); distress inks (Ranger); photo flips (Making Memories); blue cardstock; gold eyelet; color copies of game cards

On the Brink

Here Lisa used special ink made for transferring stamped and inkjet images to create her journaling passage and subtle page accent. She printed the photo and journaling passage from her inkjet printer onto regular printer paper, making sure to select the "mirror image" function in the printing menu for the text so that the transfer would not appear backward. She then laid her inkjet printout face down over her cardstock and vellum, securing each in place with removable tape. Lisa then soaked a cotton ball with the transfer ink and wet the backs of the images completely. Using another cotton ball and applying even pressure, Lisa carefully rubbed the back of the images to initiate the transfer. Once the images were transferred to her satisfaction, Lisa allowed them to dry completely before adding them to the page.

Photo: FoxFish Photography, Arvada, Colorado

TIP: Inks designed for inkjet printing and rubber stamp transfers, such as Stewart Superior's transfer ink, work well on most papers, fabrics and porous surfaces and produce a watercolor effect.

Supplies: Textured salmon and pale pink cardstocks (Bazzill); patterned papers (Design Originals, Pebbles); transfer ink (Stewart Superior); distress ink (Ranger); decorative clips (EK Success); pale pink vellum; brown and pink chalks

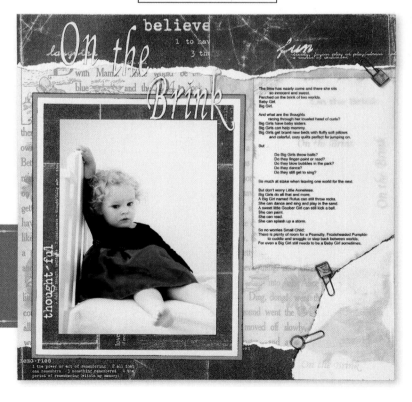

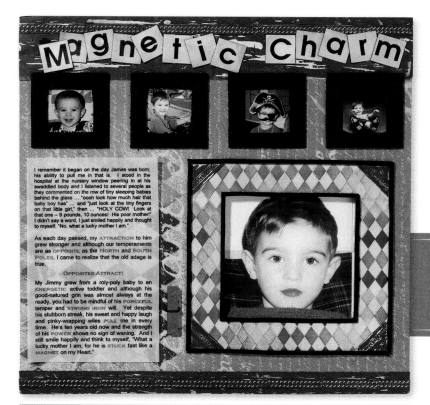

Magnetic Charm

Translate a play on words into your overall page design and choice of accents as Lisa did here. Her son's "magnetic charm" and overall "iron will" provided endless inspiration and creative opportunity in this layout. Lisa's title treatment is comprised of magnetic letters, and select words related to magnetism are highlighted in her journaling block. Lisa created a shaker box in her foam core background page and filled it with her son's photo and iron filings. When manipulated with the small accompanying magnet, the shaker makes an interactive toy reminiscent of those made popular decades ago.

TRICK: Add an interwoven theme into a journaling passage by going back over your initial draft to locate places where you can "plant" related words according to your page subject.

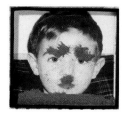

Supplies: Patterned paper (7 Gypsies); plastic mold for photo window (Plaid); leather frames, molding strips, molding corners (Making Memories); leather lace (Tejas Lace Company); acrylic paint and gesso (Delta); magnet, magnetic letters and iron filings (Lakeshore Learning); foam core board; elastic; vellum; distress inks; black pen; aluminum flashing; sandpaper

A Beautiful Mind

Here Lisa creatively displays her daughter's affinity for math with re-purposed schoolwork and bits of worksheets. These re-cycled "scratch" sheets, in combination with a paper flexagon and math game tucked into vellum and library pockets, provide perfect page additions with exponential appeal. Behind her title treatment is a tetra-tetraflexagon, or Jacob's Ladder, that when unfolded reveals Lisa's hand-written journaling.

TIP: Lisa suggests incorporating "found" journaling related to your page theme including brochures, maps, certificates, schoolwork, business cards, résumés, speeches, letters and the like.

Supplies: Patterned paper (7 Gypsies); distress inks (Ranger); library envelope (Boxer Scrapbook Productions); envelope template (Scrap Pagerz); plastic sleeve (Provo Craft); coin envelope (Staples); number stickers (Bo-Bunny Press, EK Success); coated linen thread (Scrapworks); square tags (Anima Designs); transparency letters (Carolee's Creations); word washer, snap eyelets, label holders (Making Memories); poemstone (Creative Imaginations); tangram shapes and puzzle cards (Tangoes Puzzle Game); clock hands (Walnut Hollow); washers; brads; black pen; brown pen; pumpkin cardstock; Velcro; math papers and tests

The Zack is our sweet little sleepyhead. He spends a good portion of his day napping, but that certainly doesn't stop him from sleeping soundly all night as well. You're likely to find him splayed out in front of the heating vent with the warm air blowing against his fur. If he's not there, check the living room couch. He'll either be curled up in a ball on the top or sprawled out comfortably on the throw pillows. Still can't find him? Then it's a sure bet he's snuggled up in bed next to Mom. He doesn't snore but he sure does hog the covers!

TIP: Lisa suggests using page embellishments and title treatments as creative opportunities to feature additional journaling "snippets" reflective of your page theme.

Supplies: Textured light blue and orange cardstocks (Bazzill); patterned paper (Scrapbook Wizard); clay (Provo Craft); alphabet stamps (Hero Arts); acrylic paint (Delta); metallic rub-ons (Craft T); lettering template (C-Thru Ruler); manila cardstock; mini gold eyelet; embroidery floss; brown ink; sealer

Lazybones

Journaling needn't be limited to the one-dimensional. Here Lisa incorporated words related to her journaling caption and overall page theme into eye-catching clay page accents. Lisa's clever "lazybones" title and page border were created to mimic the look of rawhide—a favorite treat of the family companion that inspired the page. An inked and matted journaling block provides endearing details.

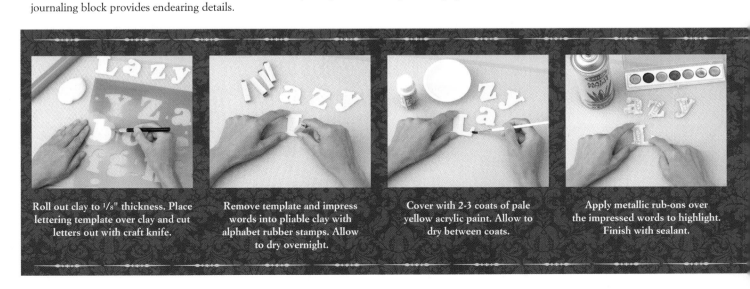

Roll out clay to 1/8" thickness. Place lettering template over clay and cut letters out with craft knife.

Remove template and impress words into pliable clay with alphabet rubber stamps. Allow to dry overnight.

Cover with 2-3 coats of pale yellow acrylic paint. Allow to dry between coats.

Apply metallic rub-ons over the impressed words to highlight. Finish with sealant.

The Littlest Grandchild

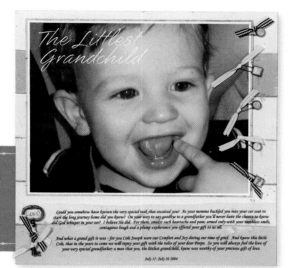

In her poignant journaling, Lisa offers a tender tribute expressing her thanks to her nephew for bringing much-needed joy to the family during a difficult time. She keeps the look of the passage understated by simply printing it onto vellum. Minimal page embellishments keep the focus on the words and emotions of the page.

Supplies: Patterned papers (Rusty Pickle, Sweetwater); metal word (DiBona Designs); decorative paper clips (EK Success); key (Westrim); natural cardstock; vellum; gingham ribbons; acrylic paint

TECHNIQUE: Tribute journaling is an effective means of articulating your appreciation for special people. Equally meaningful without accompanying photos, tribute journaling can be free-form or composed in letter, poetry and list formats detailing the individual's memorable stories, reasons he or she is loved and life accomplishments.

Sunday Best

Computer journaling printed onto fabric lends additional vintage appeal to this endearing heritage layout. To give the fabric the necessary stability to pass through her printer, Lisa ironed a 9 x 11½" fabric piece onto the shiny side of kitchen freezer paper of the same size. She then fed the paper-backed fabric through the printer and simply peeled away the paper once printing was complete. Lisa trimmed the fabric and ironed it onto a second piece using an iron-on adhesive. This no-sew "photo mat" was then embellished with cotton twine and a shoelace applied with gel glue.

TECHNIQUE: Lisa notes that she learned this deceptively simple method from her mother, an avid quilter, to create a "homespun" look while allowing her the ease and convenience of modern technology.

Supplies: Textured brown cardstock (DMD); patterned paper (Karen Foster Design); slide mount (Designer's Library); solvent ink (Tsukineko); distress ink (Ranger); letter stickers (EK Success); dimensional adhesive (JudiKins); tag (Avery); coated linen thread (Scrapworks); acid neutralizing spray (Krylon); iron-on adhesive (Therm O Web); brad; black pen; brown embroidery floss; fabric; cotton twine; cardboard; newspaper; shoelaces

A Day at the Beach

This serene seaside page is accented with quick and easy premade journaling elements. Lisa chose to feature two vellum quotes and an instant mini accordion album created from a single preprinted 12 x 12" heavyweight paper that was cut and folded. She then added her own unique touches by inking the edges of the vellum quotes and attaching them with colored tacks. Lisa embellished the album with photos and a charm-adorned jute closure and tucked it into a pocket made from coastal netting.

Supplies: Weathered cardstock (Bazzill, Paper Adventures); mini accordion album (Autumn Leaves); patterned paper (Pebbles); vellum quotes (Flair Designs); coastal netting; slide mounts (Designer's Library); rub-ons (Making Memories); colored tacks (Chatterbox); dyed twill (Scenic Route Paper Co.); seashell; sand; jute; charms; plastic tag; embroidery floss

TRICK: Utilize premade journaling products such as vellum quotes and instant albums in addition to rub-ons, letter stickers and alphabet stamps for quick and easy pages and gift albums.

I Love Your Every Thing

Because song lyrics often perfectly capture our own personal feelings and have the power to transport us back to memorable times, they provide excellent springboards for journaling. Lisa chose to feature lyrics to help articulate the many colors of her daughter's personality, which are reflected in her colorful design. For a unique page accent, Lisa included a recording of the song on compact disc along with a message to her daughter in her own handwriting.

TIP: Recall your wedding song, favorite lullaby, senior class song, first concert, favorite band and the like and include lyrics on pages that recall special memories and that reflect the words' meaning.

Supplies: Textured red paper (Bazzill); watercolor paper (Hunt Corp.); metallic foil flakes (Amy's); mini CD and case (Fuji Photo Film); poetry beads (Magnetic Poetry); watercolor pencils (Derwent); gold, teal and white cardstocks; vellum; black pen; copper wire; colored brads; silk flowers; beads

A Future Glimpse

Lisa was inspired to write a letter to her daughter containing hopes and dreams for her future based on a special photograph. Because her journaling was ultimately a personal correspondence intended for her child, Lisa concealed her emotion-rich journaling behind a hinged photo mat and highlighted select words for special emphasis.

TECHNIQUE: Using a letter format for journaling invites a natural sense of emotional disclosure, expressiveness and sincerity. Additionally, letters double as priceless heirlooms for the feelings and relationships they represent.

Supplies: Textured navy blue, light blue and green cardstocks (Bazzill, DMD); patterned papers (C-Thru Ruler); small white tag and metal-rimmed tag (Avery); dried flowers (Nature's Pressed); watch crystal (Jest Charming); brass hinges (source unknown); sheer ribbon; eyelets; gold embossing powder; black pen; pink and green chalks; floss

Who Would Guess...

Lisa incorporated self-penned poetry to express the emotions evoked by a photo from a memorable day. While excerpts from published works often make their way onto her pages, Lisa also writes her own poetry for a more artful and expressive recounting of events than can be offered by simply summing up basic photo details. Definition stickers, word stickers and documentation details complete this poetry-driven page.

TECHNIQUE: Use prose and poetry for journaling when basic names, dates and photo details don't do a special memory justice. Look to the published works of others or try your hand at harnessing your inner muse for a new approach to both creative journaling and page design.

Supplies: Red patterned paper (Deluxe Designs); acrylic word stickers (Creative Imaginations); word stickers (Bo-Bunny Press); definition sticker (Making Memories); teal, yellow, bright yellow and blue cardstocks; vellum; buttons

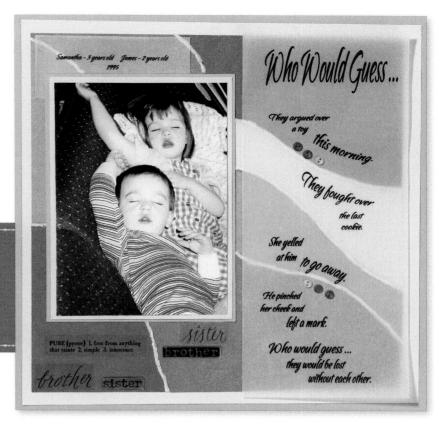

Late Night Jam Session

Etched clay board is used to feature a funky title and themed words for a fun and unique journaling treatment. Lisa first determined the placement of her title and words, then tacked a piece of white graphite paper atop the clay board. She then placed a lettering template over the transfer paper and traced the letters. Removing the transfer paper revealed the pattern, which was then traced with the point of a scratch knife. Lisa etched the inside of the letters to remove the black coating using the flat edge of the scratch knife, applying gentle strokes to control the amount of exposed white clay beneath. Color was then added with colored pencils.

TIP: Clay board is a board or heavy cardstock coated with a chalky white clay material beneath a black topcoat. It is available in textures, including pebble, linen and canvas and also comes in white, rainbow and holographic varieties.

Supplies: Textured blue cardstock (DMD, Paper Adventures); clay board (Ampersand Art Supply); labels (Dymo); die cuts (Meri Meri); lettering template (Frances Meyer); red and yellow cardstocks; red and yellow chalks; colored pencils; guitar picks; strings; string packet; guitar tablatures (downloaded from Internet)

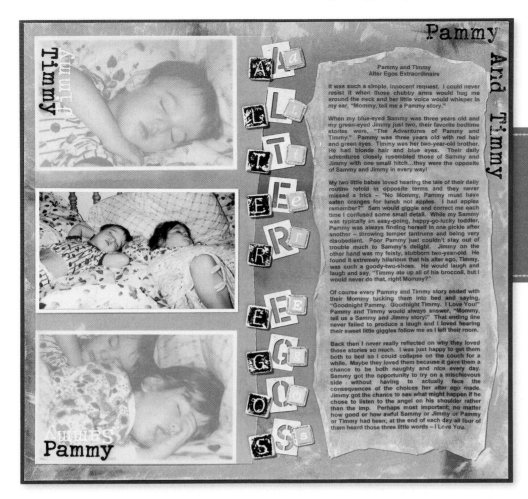

Pammy And Timmy

Timmy

Pammy

Sammy
Pammy

A L T E R E G O S S

Pammy and Timmy
Alter Egos Extraordinaire

It was such a simple, innocent request. I could never resist it when those chubby arms would hug me around the neck and her little voice would whisper in my ear, "Mommy, tell me a Pammy story."

When my blue-eyed Sammy was three years old and my green-eyed Jimmy just two, their favorite bedtime stories were, "The Adventures of Pammy and Timmy." Pammy was three years old with red hair and green eyes. Timmy was her two-year-old brother. He had blonde hair and blue eyes. Their daily adventures closely resembled those of Sammy and Jimmy with one small hitch...they were the opposite of Sammy and Jimmy in every way!

My two little babes loved hearing the tale of their daily routine retold in opposite terms and they never missed a trick – "No Mommy, Pammy must have eaten oranges for lunch not apples. I had apples remember?" Sam would giggle and correct me each time I confused some small detail. While my Sammy was typically an easy-going, happy-go-lucky toddler, Pammy was always finding herself in one pickle after another – throwing temper tantrums and being very disobedient. Poor Pammy just couldn't stay out of trouble much to Sammy's delight. Jimmy on the other hand was my feisty, stubborn two-year-old. He found it extremely hilarious that his alter ego, Timmy, was such a goody-two-shoes. He would laugh and laugh and say, "Timmy ate up all of his broccoli, but I would never do that, right Mommy?"

Of course every Pammy and Timmy story ended with their Mommy tucking them into bed and saying, "Goodnight Pammy. Goodnight Timmy. I Love You!" Pammy and Timmy would always answer, "Mommy, tell us a Sammy and Jimmy story!" That ending line never failed to produce a laugh and I loved hearing their sweet little giggles follow me as I left their room.

Back then I never really reflected on why they loved those stories so much. I was just happy to get them both to bed so I could collapse on the couch for a while. Maybe they loved them because it gave them a chance to be both naughty and nice every day. Sammy got the opportunity to try on a mischievous side without having to actually face the consequences of the choices her alter ego made. Jimmy got the chance to see what might happen if he chose to listen to the angel on his shoulder rather than the imp. Perhaps most important; no matter how good or how awful Sammy or Jimmy or Pammy or Timmy had been; at the end of each day all four of them heard those three little words – I Love You.

TECHNIQUE: Gel transfers can also be done with handwritten journaling and may be enhanced with colored pens and whimsical doodles and designs. For computer journaling, use multiple fonts and colors of ink for visual interest.

Supplies: Textured purple cardstock (Bazzill); patterned paper (Creative Imaginations); gloss gel medium (Liquitex); black tile letters (Westrim); letter brads (Colorbök); rub-ons (Making Memories); alphabet punch out letters (Scrapworks); black and white acrylic paints

Alter Egos

Lisa recounted her children's love of hearing the adventures of characters that resemble themselves from a favorite bedtime book. By using a gel medium to transfer her journaling, Lisa created a passage that looks as though it was pulled straight from the pages of the storybook. Once the process was complete, Lisa attached the element to her page alongside endearing photos.

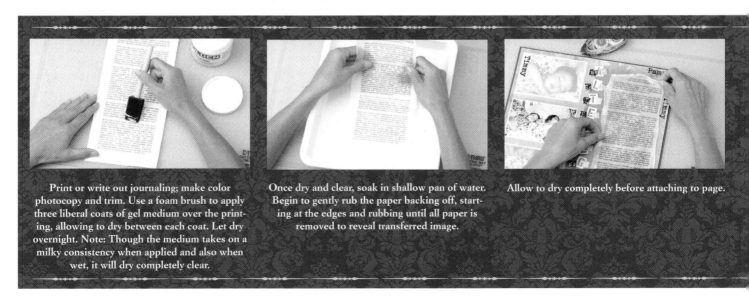

Print or write out journaling; make color photocopy and trim. Use a foam brush to apply three liberal coats of gel medium over the printing, allowing to dry between each coat. Let dry overnight. Note: Though the medium takes on a milky consistency when applied and also when wet, it will dry completely clear.

Once dry and clear, soak in shallow pan of water. Begin to gently rub the paper backing off, starting at the edges and rubbing until all paper is removed to reveal transferred image.

Allow to dry completely before attaching to page.

Look for a Rainbow

In this clever layout, Lisa's page theme of looking beyond the obvious to find the positive is represented in both her journaling and her page design. A rainbow-inspired motivational quote perfectly articulated Lisa's experience of encouraging her son to look on the bright side when rain postponed a trip to the park. Lisa "planted" a paraphrasing of the quote by first writing her journaling and then reworking portions of it to incorporate key words needed to form the phrase. She then printed the passage onto vellum and highlighted each word with pieces of white paper affixed to the backside.

Supplies: Clay (Polyform Products); transfer paper (Hewlett Packard); black and white cardstocks; colored inks; vellum; black pen; colored brads; cheesecloth

TECHNIQUE: Use this impressive method when you have lengthy journaling passages. quotes, lyrics and the like may be used for hidden messages or you may wish to compose your own sentiment. Changing the size, color and font of the key words is an additional creative means for "revealing" them.

Bazooka Jim Gets Pink Eye

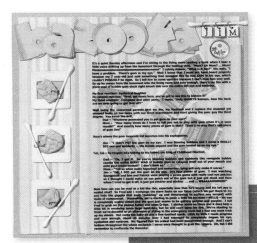

Instead of allowing a humorous family fiasco to fade into distant memory, Lisa remedied the predicament of not having photographic "evidence" by recalling the event in a highly detailed and engaging narrative. By incorporating the five senses and including dialogue, Lisa paints a picture with words that ultimately renders accompanying photos unnecessary. The passage was printed onto vellum and is layered over Bazooka wrappers. Realistic polymer clay "gum wads" and cotton swabs provide pseudo memorabilia to resemble the means by which Lisa removed a chewing gum eye patch from the face of her bewildered son.

Supplies: Patterned paper (Scrapbook Wizard); polymer clay (Polyform Products); gloss gel medium (Liquitex); letter tiles (Junkitz); metal-rimmed tag, square jump rings (Making Memories); lettering template (Scrap Pagerz); pink cardstock; vellum; slide mounts; black pen; acrylic paint; chalk; pink brad; cotton swabs; gum wrappers

TECHNIQUE: Photoless memories need not be absent from scrapbooks. Whether you find yourself out of film, without your camera completely or in a situation where photos are not allowed, sketches and scribbled notes can suffice until an opportunity to document all the details arises. Memorabilia can help offset the absence of supporting photos.

An Ocean Apart

Lisa featured scans of photos and the messages hand-penned on their backs for a nostalgic journaling treatment. Given by her mother-in-law to her future husband stationed overseas, the charming sentiments deliver added emotion to the layout. Lisa printed the photos and messages onto off-white cardstock and trimmed the edges with deckle-edged scissors to mimic old-style photos. She then paired each sentiment with its respective photo and tucked each into a bulletin board element comprised of vintage-themed papers, ribbon and gold brads. Additional computer printed journaling provides further detail.

Supplies: Patterned paper (Anna Griffin, Pebbles); ribbon corners (Anna Griffin); tags (Avery); heart stamp (All Night Media); letter eyelets (Making Memories); metal letters (Colorbök); metallic rub-ons (Craft-T); letter stickers (EK Success); green cardstock; sheer ribbon; gold brads; photo corners; pink, gold, green and blue inks; embossing powder; embossing ink pen; bronze and green acrylic paints; heart charms; cross-stitched

TRICK: Incorporating handwriting from the backs of photos adds a special touch to a page as well as ready-made journaling, and works particularly well for heritage layouts.

The Worldly Wisdom of a Boy

When distanced by time, your child's mayhem, mishaps and silly misadventures take on new and humorous meaning, inspiring just as many thoughts of nostalgia as more sentimental journaling passages. In this layout, Lisa incorporated a collection of her young son's finest moments at the time this angelic photo was taken. In addition to her tender and reflective journaling block, Lisa created a multifold booklet to house lessons both she and her son learned the hard way that now put her into hysterics.

TECHNIQUE: In addition to allowing for a substantial amount of journaling on a single page, Lisa's booklet is particularly effective because its unassuming contents so endearingly contradict of the sweetness of the photo. Including humor in sentimental journaling with just-the-right presentation is an engaging and unique approach to capturing memories.

Supplies: Patterned paper, slide mount (Design Originals); printable canvas (Burlington); watch crystal (Jest Charming); dimensional adhesive (JudiKins); coated linen thread (Scrapworks); word tag (Hot Off The Press); die cut letters (Sizzix); metallic rub-ons (Craf-T); distress ink (Ranger); cream cardstock; vellum; transparency; black pen

Let the Beauty We Love...

Here Lisa used a favorite quote as a title treatment that she first came across in a greeting card. For its special significance, Lisa wanted to incorporate the sentiment as a page element and to also inspire the journaling passage detailing her feelings of being a stay-at-home mom. Watercolor pencils lend an elegant touch to the script title while creative text placement and matting make for an eye-catching journaling block.

TECHNIQUE: Include the reasoning of your love for, and personal connection to, meaningful quotes and sayings for emotionally charged journaling and title treatments.

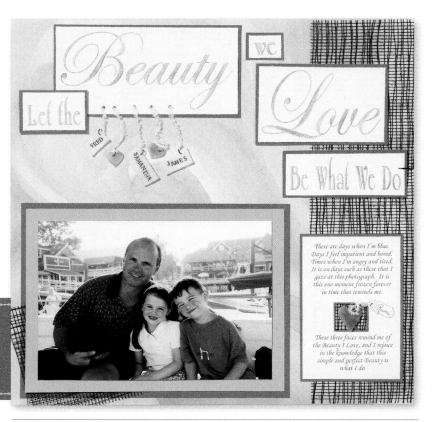

Supplies: Patterned paper (Creative Imaginations); shrink plastic (Duncan); rubber stamps (Hero Arts); mesh (Magenta); watercolor pencils (Derwent); jump rings (Nicole); mini eyelets (Making Memories); black ink; blue pen; blue and light blue cardstocks; fibers

Face It

With this deceptively straightforward page, Lisa created a title that changes through the use of an interactive journaling feature. By opening up the accordion-folded "embellishment" at the bottom right corner, all but "face it" becomes covered, revealing various physical attributes that each complete the title sentence in a new way. Lisa tucked handwritten tags detailing her love for her son's characteristics into the booklet, which is secured closed with snap tape.

TECHNIQUE: Utilize this "dual title" technique as a means of incorporating several pictures and words onto one page or a two-page spread, all the while making for a fun interactive element that works well with several themes.

Supplies: Patterned papers, die-cut frames (KI Memories); round metal letters (Treasured Memories); square metal letters, metal-rimmed tag (Making Memories); magnetic words (Magnetic Poetry); coin envelopes (Staples); tags (Avery); alphabet stamps (Hero Arts); snap tape, cotton twine, green cardstock, vellum; black pen; black ink; aqua ink

A Christmas Tree Is

To complement her twinkling Christmas tree photo, Lisa chose to feature an assortment of single words and short phrases that the scene inspired. For visual interest, she entered her text into a word processing document and selected "word art" to manipulate direction, placement, size and font. She then printed the assortment onto green vellum that was then mounted over a slightly smaller piece of yellow patterned paper.

TECHNIQUE: Jump-start your own journaling with this quick and easy technique. Briefly look at your photos, then immediately write down a list of thoughts and feelings that the photos inspire, allowing each word and statement to help inspire the next.

Supplies: Patterned papers (Karen Foster Design, Magenta); mesh paper (Magenta); metal-rimmed tags (Avery); jewelry caps (Nicole); glitter (PSX Design); cardstock; green vellum; gold wire; green and gold embossing powders

Kathy FESMIRE

COLOR

Kathy became a scrapbooker after the hobby was selected as the craft of the month at a local organization to which she belonged. Before long, she had completed a gift album for her parents and was hard at work compiling another for her daughter. Seven years later, Kathy continues to create layouts intended for the family that inspires them.

Having an art background has allowed Kathy to incorporate the principles and elements of design into her layouts, most notably represented in her striking signature use of color. While Kathy looks to her featured photos to drive the palette of her pages, she goes a step further to ensure her combinations are eye-catching. "The first step to understanding color is to purchase a color wheel and use it! I have a large color wheel that I keep in my scrapbook room and a small one to take with me to stores and on crop retreats." Instead of habitually calling upon favorite tried-and-true colors, Kathy looks to the hues reflected in clothing, home décor, nature and print media to inspire a new spectrum of options. "You can find color combinations that work well together almost everywhere you look. Open your mind along with your eyes and look for color combinations that you might never have thought of on your own."

Kathy divides her time between freelance artwork and scrapbook designing in addition to her job as an art teacher. She lives in Athens, Tennessee, with husband Austin and four children, Alex, Morgan, Hayden and Isaac.

Pickin' Up Chicks

Departing from the typical process of choosing colors and themes limited to those represented in the photo, Kathy essentially "started from scratch" by removing all color but that of the chick's. Eliminating the busy background and distracting colors allowed Kathy to create a country theme—a far cry from the bustling classroom captured in the photo. A red barn, golden bales of hay, a whitewashed fence and gingham tablecloths are evoked in the strategic color choices and embellishments used.

TECHNIQUE: Employ this unique approach to color by strategically altering photos to black-and-white with the exception of select elements to give them focus. Doing so opens up limitless possibilities to create page themes based on colors of your choosing.

Supplies: Paisley patterned paper (Flair Designs); crackle patterned paper (source unknown); straw patterned paper (Daisy D's); hinges, twill and chicken wire sticker (Creek Bank Creations); rub-ons and safety pins (Making Memories); wooden tags (Karen's Crafts); small tag and journaling tag (Pebbles); alphabet stamps (Plaid); foam fence sticker (source unknown); chick stickers (Sandylion); alphabet stickers (EK Success); library pocket (Designer's Library); brads; gingham ribbon; jute ribbon; embroidery floss; black and red cardstocks; ink

Animal Kingdom

Here Kathy made her color choices based on the safari theme evoked by her photos. Rich, dark brown papers, earthy-hued animal prints, black stitching and glossy tiger's eye beads combine to support her page theme in a striking way.

TIP: Break from the tendency of pulling dominant, obvious colors present in photos to dictate your design choices and instead look to play up a particular theme through the use of color and accents.

Supplies: Linen paper (Flair Designs); faux wood patterned paper (Pebbles); animal print paper, leather frames (Making Memories); rust patterned paper (Karen Foster Design); letter stickers (EK Success, Pebbles, Wordsworth); labels (Dymo); tiger's eye beads (Expo International); animal bookmarks (source unknown); ink; dark brown, brown and tan papers; embroidery floss

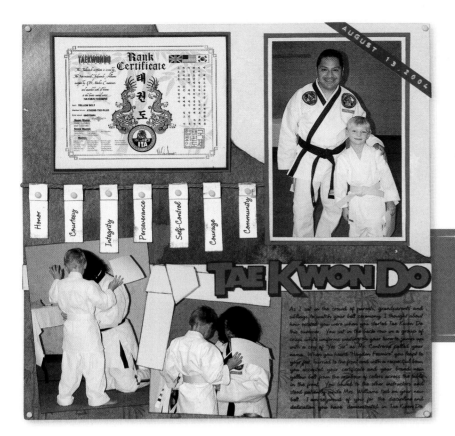

Tae Kwon Do

The colors Kathy chose on this spread commemorating her son's accomplishment in Tae Kwon Do practically pop off the page. Red, blue and yellow are a representation of a triadic color scheme, which is formed based on equal distances between colors on the color wheel. Since her photos didn't contain a great deal of color, Kathy called on scans of her son's rank certificate and the title element of a flier announcing the event to inspire her selections.

TECHNIQUE: Locating triadic schemes using a color wheel is as easy as counting. The key is the equal distance between the colors, which guarantees an eye-pleasing, page-popping combination.

Supplies: Yellow faux-textured paper (Paper Adventures); yellow wash paper (EK Success); red wash paper (Provo Craft); blue wash paper (Wordsworth); labels (Dymo); bamboo stamp (DeNami Design Rubber Stamps); transparency; fiber; brads; ink

Big Brown Eyes

Few color combinations are as eye-catching as a primary scheme of red, yellow and blue. Kathy's page works especially well because not only do the colors represent those in the photo, but also because primaries are cheerful, vibrant and ultimately perfect for kid pages. A polka-dot patterned background is layered with torn sections of solid and patterned papers. Metal-rimmed tags were given red, blue and yellow centers and red gingham ribbon. Oversized brads lend additional visual appeal.

TRICK: Red, blue and yellow, along with black and white, are used to mix every other color that exists! Moreover, these colors cannot be mixed by combining any other colors, making them the true heart of the color wheel.

Supplies: Patterned papers (Paper Patch, Stamping Station); metal-rimmed tags, brands (Making Memories); heart accent (EK Success); letter stickers (Wordsworth); letter stamps (Printworks, PSX Design, Stampendous!, Wordsworth); blue, yellow and red papers; vellum; ribbon; keys; ink; pen; embroidery floss

WHAT I WANT YOU TO KNOW

AS YOU LEAVE FOR

ALEX, I AM SO PROUD OF YOU YOUR beauty IS INSIDE & OUT YOUR faith INSPIRES ME YOUR heart IS KIND & GOOD YOUR smile MAKES ME HAPPY

A season of change

college

AUG 04

TIP: As Kathy demonstrates, various shades of each color in a diad combination can be successfully incorporated into a page's design.

Supplies: Blue watermark paper, rub-on letters, metal-rimmed tags (Making Memories); letter stamps (Plaid); file folder (Esselte); charm (Create A Craft); blue paper, ribbon, ink; clips

What I Want You to Know...

Wanting to keep the focus on the photo and not compete with the pattern of her stepdaughter's shirt, Kathy again looked to her color wheel for just-the-right combination. What she settled on was a diad, or a combination of two colors that are two spaces apart on the color wheel. Vibrant blues and purples represented in her choices of paper, a file folder, ribbon and ink make for a winning combination.

Use premade tag or ruler to trace a tag shape at the upper edge of a piece of cardstock; cut to desired width. Fold the paper down to the traced edge of the tag.

Accordion-fold the paper to the tag's width and trim any excess. Use a hole punch to make a hole through all layers.

Using a multicolored stamp pad, stamp each tag, matching the colors to make a continuous color strip on each. Add a hole reinforcer on each tag and add journaling as desired.

Bug Hunt

The striking colors on this page work not only because they pull from colors in the photos, but also because they represent an analogous color scheme. Analogous colors consist of three to five colors that are located side by side on the color wheel. The rich shades of green and blue are associated with grass, water and all things outdoors—perfect for a page dedicated to scouting for summertime bugs! Kathy's vibrant ribbon accents, stamped papers and silk leaves create a cheerful and eye-appealing combination.

Supplies: Patterned papers (Bo-Bunny Press, Magenta); library pocket and card (Gaylord); alphabet and number stamps (Plaid); dragonfly stamp (Stampin' Up!); rub-on letters (Making Memories); die-cut letters (Sizzix); blue paper; blue-violet paper; dark blue paper; black cardstock; various ribbon; ink; colored pencils; safety pins

TIP: Calling on analogous colors schemes is perhaps the easiest and most foolproof way of ensuring that your color combination will be a success. Simply locate one color from your photos on the color wheel and add a handful of immediately neighboring hues.

H_2O

After seeing these playful pool-time photos, Kathy knew the scrapbook page to follow would incorporate a cool color scheme of blues, greens and purples. Taking from the colors of her daughter's swimsuit, the water and some very popular purple goggles, Kathy color-blocked her page background with patterned papers and added a strung oversized-bead border page divider. Coordinating papers provided mats for each photo, and were also used to wrap and back the letter stencils used in the title treatment.

Supplies: Wavy striped paper, blue wash paper (Paper Adventures); violet, yellow-green paper (Karen Foster Design); teal, blue diamond and blue square papers (Creative Imaginations); oversized beads (Beadery); number sticker (Doodlebug Design); rub-on letters, numbers, staples and ribbon photo corners (Making Memories); alphabet stencils (Wal-Mart); eyelets

TECHNIQUE: Kathy's winning color combination was comprised by dividing the color wheel in half vertically. The cool colors are represented from yellow-green through the blues to violet.

Sleeping Beauty

Instead of feeling compelled to create a layout of pinks to showcase photos of a sleeping baby girl, Kathy opted to use muted shades of blue for the soothing feeling they evoke. Various blue ribbons, stamped twill, silk flowers and mini file folder accents blend beautifully with three different patterned papers. Silver hinges and a circle tag are also in keeping with the cool colors of the layout.

Photos: FoxFish Photography, Arvada, Colorado

Supplies: Floral patterned papers (Provo Craft); gingham patterned paper (Sandylion); mini file folders, twill, hinges, circle tag (Creek Bank Creations); rub-on words (Making Memories); letter stickers (Wordsworth); silk flowers; brads eyelets; various ribbon

TIP: Look beyond the sex of a child and typical baby accents as Kathy did here to instead create a mood with strategic color choices for the feelings they represent.

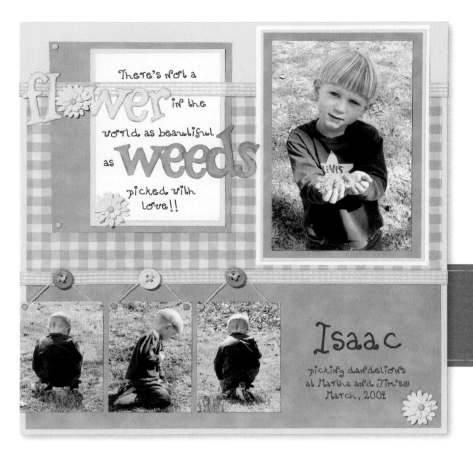

...Weeds Picked With Love

This page is a perfect example of pulling colors from your photos to dictate your color scheme. Kathy picked one predominant color from the photos (green) and one secondary color (yellow) for her color combination. She then selected a third "neutral" color (white) that would not compete with the others. Together the papers and accents combine harmoniously and keep the emphasis on the photos of Kathy's son and his heartfelt, handpicked bouquet.

TIP: Utilize multipatterned, monochromatic packs of paper and accompanying accents from the same manufacturer to help ensure exact color matches to pull a page together in a flash.

Supplies: Patterned papers (Making Memories); punched flowers (Carl, Family Treasures); letter die cuts (Sizzix); white cardstock; green and yellow buttons; yellow and green papers; gingham ribbon; brads; black chalk; yellow embroidery floss

Egg Hunt

When Kathy saw how nicely the red-violet dress her daughter was wearing popped against the green grass in the photo, she knew it had to be a color combination on the color wheel. After locating the two colors on the wheel, she noticed that if yellow was added to the red-violet and green color scheme it would become what is known as a split-complementary. The colors of Kathy's color-blocked page background all represent variations on this eye-pleasing combination, as do the acrylic-paint-treated letters and journaling block. To give the egg accents and letters a little sheen, Kathy applied a coat of crystal lacquer.

TRICK: When you see colors that look particularly attractive together in your photos, use your color wheel to form a split-complementary. Start with a color you wish to use, then locate its complement directly across from it on the color wheel. This color, and those to either side, form a split-complementary.

Supplies: Patterned papers (Colorbök, Jane, Scrap In A Snap); green dot paper (Current); rub-on letters (Making Memories); sun die cut (Sizzix); wooden letters (Crafts, Etc.); crystal lacquer (Sakura Hobby Craft); red-violet and green papers; white and yellow cardstocks; green, eyelets; ribbon; brads; acrylic paint; transparency

Rainforest Café

This jungle-inspired page is another example of a split-complementary color scheme. Here a nontraditional color combination was just what this layout called for, and was devised by locating the red color of the bird in the photo on the color wheel and finding its complement (green). The blue-green and yellow-green colors to either side of the complementary popped when paired with the red and the many hues represented in the photo. Kathy accented her solid and patterned papers with ribbon accents and leather flowers for an unexpected, striking final result.

TIP: Kathy suggests incorporating "neutral" tones like black, white or gray into your layouts to accent your color combinations without competing against them. Here splashes of black work well as an addition to this eye-pleasing combination.

Supplies: Flower patterned paper (Colors by Design); yellow-green patterned paper (Magenta); rub-on word, leather flowers, staples, alphabet stamp (Making Memories); sticker numbers (Bo-Bunny Press); yellow-green, red and blue-green papers; ink; acrylic paint; various ribbons

Green Eggs and Hands

Kathy chose a green monochromatic color scheme to play off both her whimsical title and the colors in the photos. Multitonal patterned papers layered over a solid background are embellished with buttons, various ribbons and a green-centered metal-rimmed tag for a fun take on an egg-dying experience.

TRICK: Kathy didn't depart from her monochromatic color scheme of green by bringing in black accents. Monochromatic color schemes are comprised of one color along with black and white.

Supplies: Patterned papers, metal-rimmed tag (Making Memories); alphabet stamps (PSX Design); black, white and green cardstocks; ink; various ribbons; buttons

Supplies: Patterned papers (Creative Imaginations, Doodlebug Design, Memories in the Making); labels (Dymo); rub-on words (Making Memories); discs (Jest Charming); red cardstock; ribbon; yellow brads; ink

Beach Boys

Kathy re-created the heat felt on a day at the beach with colors considered "warm" on the color wheel. Warm colors are those between red-violet moving clockwise down to yellow, and communicate intensity much like temperature. The ribbon accents and patterned paper title mat both mimic the boys' flame-inspired swim trunks while dot-patterned paper and plastic discs creatively represent the sun.

Cut white cardstock into 2½ x 3½" rectangles, one for each letter. Mix ⅔ of package of non-sweetened Kool-Aid with ¼ cup water in a small bowl. Immerse and let sit until desired color is achieved. Alternate colors for every other rectangle. Remove and let dry completely on paper towels.

Mix remaining ⅓ of package of Kool-Aid into bowls with a small amount of the original Kool-Aid solution. Using a straw, draw concentrated Kool-Aid and splatter onto colored rectangles to create darker areas; let dry.

Using a pencil, draw or trace letters from template onto strips, alternating colors; cut out. Chalk the edges first with chalk the same color as your paper, then black.

Ink the edges in black ink. When all letters are finished, you may spray with Archival Mist if desired.

Ladybugs

This page showcasing the enchantment provided by a tiny winged wonder packs a great deal of visual punch. It is another example of a complementary color scheme, except this time utilizes much more intense, or bright shades of blue and orange. Here boldly colored papers, ribbon, fibers, brads, and even label stickers are perfectly paired to demonstrate this concept.

Supplies: Orange patterned paper (Scrappy Cat); metal-rimmed tags, oversized orange brads (Making Memories); labels (Dymo); charm (Create-A-Craft); letter die cut (Sizzix); orange, white and blue cardstocks; fibers; ribbon

TIP: Kathy advises resisting the tendency to limit color options based on the most popular choices for a certain topic (in this case, red and black for ladybugs). Instead, try using the color wheel to help guide you in a direction that might be different from the norm, but a perfect fit for your page.

Pumpkin Picasso

Kathy's dimensional background comprised of numerous cut and inked patterned paper squares is an example of a complementary color scheme, which means the colors are located directly across from one another on the color wheel. Complementary color combinations are a surefire way to strike an eye-pleasing balance each and every time. Here deeper shades of blue were used for the page background, tag accents and title treatment, while varying degrees of orange and cream comprise the other accents. Kathy's emphasis on squares throughout her design is a clever nod to Picasso's paintings in the early years of his cubist period.

Supplies: Patterned papers (Bo-Bunny Press, Karen Foster Design, Pebbles); alphabet stamps (Making Memories); letter and number stickers (EK Success); "Picasso" signature (downloaded from Internet); orange acrylic paint; brads; navy paper; cream paper; buttons; pen

TIP: A color's intensity refers to its brightness or dullness, of which each individual color has in varying degrees. Deeper shades are more dull while brighter shades have a higher intensity. Be sure to choose not only the right colors for your layout, but the levels of intensity that best enhance the photos and overall feel of the layout.

I'm Crabby!

The red hues throughout this layout help to emphasize the frustration evident in this pull-at-your-heartstings photo of one unhappy little boy. When combined with playful crab accents, the intense and warm color value of red was perfect for poking a little fun at an otherwise dramatic moment. By altering the photo to emphasize the blue of the denim overalls, Kathy was able to maintain total control over the color choices for the layout to best create feeling using color.

Supplies: Faux wood patterned paper (Hot Off The Press); faux linen patterned paper (source unknown); corrugated paper (DMD); small paper crabs (EK Success); die-cut letters (Sizzix); slide mount (Keller's Creations); staples (Making Memories); crab wineglass charm (Wal-Mart); red and tans cardstocks; button; twine; fish net; handmade paper pieced crab; tag; chalk; stamping ink; acrylic paint

TIP: Consider colors for your layouts based on the emotion evoked by your photo subject. Warm colors such as red can be used to represent intensity.

We've Been Flamingoed

Kathy wanted to chronicle a humorous church fund-raising prank with a fun layout. The brilliant pink of the kitschy pink lawn flamingoes against the green grass inspired her bold color choices. She created her own flamingo paper piecing with paint, ink and chalk. Paint was also applied to a diamond stamp to alter harlequin patterned paper, while a thin brush was used to apply stripes to pink crackle-patterned paper. Eyelets, metal-rimmed tags, ribbon, silk flowers and label stickers continue the color scheme.

TECHNIQUE: As Kathy demonstrates, you needn't always take patterned papers at face value. Artfully enhance their color or design with painting, inking and stamps to really make a statement.

Supplies: Patterned papers (source unknown); label stickers (Dymo); metal-rimmed tags, alphabet and date stamps (Making Memories); die-cut letters (Sizzix); silk flowers; brads; eyelets; pink, black and white cardstocks; ribbon; homemade diamond stamp

A Conversation With Isaac at 4

After altering a photo to remove its busy background and color, Kathy knew this charming photo of her son would be a perfect complement to a silly conversation she was wanting to scrapbook. Consequently her achromatic color scheme, or use of black, white and shades of gray, was conceived. Several patterned papers and dimensional accents combine for a collage-style layout comprised of stark contrasts.

TIP: Make sure to use varying shades of gray and areas of pure black and white to create contrast in your pages. Kathy's white mat with a black edge against the text patterned paper is an example of good contrast.

Supplies: Patterned papers (Current, DMD, Tumbleweed); printed tag, mini brads, rub-ons (Making Memories); hinges (Creek Bank Creations); house numbers (Cole, HyKo); letter stickers (Bo-Bunny Press, Sandylion, Wordsworth); sticker numbers (Chatterbox, Pebbles); wooden letters (Crafts, Etc.); white tag (DMD); labels (Dymo); black and white cardstocks; ribbon; rickrack; acrylic paint; safety pins; domino

Hayden Gets His Cast Off

Once Kathy got a glimpse of these photos, she knew she had a great page to play out a secondary color scheme. Secondary colors (green, orange, violet or purple) are created by mixing two of the primary colors together, such as combining yellow and blue to make green. The purple from the cast, green from the playground slide and orange from the boys' shirts dictated Kathy's choices in fun patterned papers and whimsical notions. She added layers of purple paint-treated mesh to an inked letter stencil to mimic the look of the cast, and cut another letter stencil from purple textured paper.

TIP: Since the purple was the least shown secondary color in the photos, Kathy used a larger percentage of it on the page to make the color pop. Work to pull out small splashes of color in your own photos that can be brought out by elements in the page.

Supplies: Patterned papers (Bo-Bunny Press, Deluxe Designs, Stamping Station); rub-on words, alphabet and date stamps, metal-rimmed tags (Making Memories); dome epoxy letter stickers (Creative Imaginations); letter stencil (Creek Bank Creations); large letter stencil (Office Depot); mesh (Magic Mesh); white cardstock; various ribbon; rickrack; brads; buttons; acrylic paint; ink; embroidery floss

Lava Lava Island

Here again Kathy let the color wheel do some of the page planning where her colors were concerned. This island-inspired layout is comprised of tertiary colors, or colors made by mixing a primary color with a secondary color. The bright and tropical appearance of the colors perfectly coordinated with the beach scene backdrop. Kathy added additional bursts of color with whimsical patterned papers, layered title letters and striking monochromatic flower accents with embroidery threaded centers. The hula skirt-inspired page border introduces a neutral color in addition to enhancing the page theme.

Photos: Home Run Photography, Englewood, Tennessee

TECHNIQUE: Kathy's flower border accents were hand drawn onto paper, cut out, then given detail and depth with pen, ink and chalk. For the centers, Kathy poked small holes in the centers and also at three different heights, which were then stitched with embroidery floss and knotted at each end.

Supplies: Patterned papers (Imagination Project, Paper Adventures, Stamping Station) title letter stencils (C-Thru Ruler); metal-rimmed tags (Making Memories); labels (Dymo); letter stickers and numbers (Wordsworth); alphabet stamps (Plaid); leaf die cut (Sizzix); blue-green, dark blue-green and gray cardstocks; chalk; black pen; black ink; embroidery thread; raffia, handmade flowers

Angie HEAD

Interactive Elements

Angie became a scrapbooker six years ago after being introduced to the craft through a local crop. Intrigued by the concept of telling stories with photos and inspired by all of the product and supplies, it wasn't long before Angie was hooked and attending crops on a weekly basis.

As Angie's scrapbooking skills evolved, so did her approach to photography. In order to experiment and improve, Angie soon found that she had more shots representing each event and occasion than she could ever hope to chronicle in her scrapbooks. As a result, Angie began devising the interactive elements that have become her hallmark in order to feature several photos on a single page or spread. "I will normally enlarge the best photo to use as my focal point and then I will incorporate interactive elements to reveal as many pictures as possible of that event, as well as journaling." In addition to the functionality of interactive elements, Angie enjoys them for the spontaneity they lend to her layouts and for the way they actively draw the viewer into the page. "I love little surprises, unexpected gifts, homes with nooks and crannies, junk drawers and all sorts of hidden trinkets and treasures. I have found interactive elements give me a way to bring my love of these things into my scrapbooking."

In addition to her scrapbooking endeavors, Angie is a home-schooling mother. She lives in Friendswood, Texas, with husband Scott and children Caleb and Callie.

What a Difference a Day Can Make

Here Angie featured a photo of her daughter on her last day as a 3-year-old alongside a photo ushering in her first day as a 4-year-old, creatively capturing the transition between baby and little girl. Angie cleverly incorporated two small handwritten journaling cards adorned with painted number stencil covers. By securing each closed with photo turns, Angie's unassuming and artful page accents double as interactive elements.

TECHNIQUE: Angie created her journaling cards by mounting the number stencils on cardstock twice the size of the stencil itself. She then scored the cardstock on the left-hand edge of the stencil to create the fold, trimming away the excess cardstock. After completing her journaling, Angie adorned each with number stickers and painted metal accents.

Supplies: Patterned papers (Scrappy Cat); number stencils, tags (Avery); letter stickers (Chatterbox, Scrapbook Wizard, SEI); snaps (Chatterbox); metal letters and numbers, metal-rimmed tag, paper flowers, flower brads, photo turns, label holder, metal word (Making Memories); fibers; metallic rubons; acrylic paint

My Mornings With You

Nothing takes attention away from the engaging photo of Angie's daughter in this layout. Angie was able to adorn her page with several tactile accents, including chenille fabric, ribbons, buttons and paper flowers, without forfeiting room for an interactive journaling element. Discreetly tucked beneath the double-matted photo is a handwritten cardstock journaling card adorned with ribbon.

TIP: This pull-out journaling card can be created in a snap and could be crafted in an array of sizes and shapes. Simply ink the edges and punch three small holes along the top, tie with ribbon, and tuck behind a photo or into a pocket for a subtle page addition.

Supplies: Patterned paper (Me & My Big Ideas); sticker (Memories Complete); alphabet stamps (River City Rubber Works); paper flowers, straight pins, molding corner (Making Memories); yellow and white cardstocks; chenille fabric; hat pin; buttons; acrylic paint; ink; ribbons

Callie

This shabby chic-inspired page features a flip-style photo booklet. Distressed metal hinges complement Callie's crocheted hat and invite the viewer to see what's behind the cover photo. Angie created the booklet's pages by mounting photos on both sides of cut cardstock and accenting with rub-on words or metal art accents. The final page contains vellum-printed journaling mounted over inked patterned paper.

TRICK: Angie used the metal hinges as a template to craft two additional hinges from chipboard. These secondary hinges were mounted beneath the metal ones and sandwiched between the second and third pages of the booklet.

Supplies: Embroidered paper (Provo Craft); textured pink paper (Magenta); hinges (EK Success); metal art (K & Company); alphabet stickers (Creative Imaginations); floral stickers (K & Company, Memories Complete); paper flowers, label holder, rub-on words (Making Memories); tag (Avery); white cardstock; vellum; pink brads; lace; ribbon; ink; foam adhesive

Callie and Karoline

Angie used an envelope template to create a place to tuck her photo tag element. Several cropped photos were mounted on both sides of cardstock cut to fit inside the envelope. A reproduction vintage tag was accented with an eyelet and personalized with the names of the two girls for the cover. Ribbon was then threaded through small holes punched in the top of each "page" and joined to the cover with knotted green ribbon.

Photos: Family Memories, Friendswood, Texas

TIP: Envelopes aren't just for sending cards through the mail. Make use of the wide array of templates available for housing photos, journaling and memorabilia on a page. You can easily customize your creations according to the size and shape of the envelope you desire.

Supplies: Patterned paper (Autumn Leaves); reproduction vintage ephemera tag (Me & My Big Ideas); concho (Scrapworks); square brads (Making Memories); vellum; double-sided paper; organza

TIP: In addition to housing photo and journaling cards, this envelope accent would be ideal for keeping memorabilia or small bound booklets.

Supplies: Textured black cardstock (Bazzill); patterned vellum (American Crafts); envelope template (Deluxe Designs); text sticker (Cloud 9 Design); small and large alphabet stamps, metal plaque, rub-on word, label holders (Making Memories); pink paper; pink tulle; silk flower; gingham ribbon; pink acrylic paint; black ink

Forever Friends

Using an envelope template and patterned vellum, Angie created an eye-catching page accent to house several additional photos. Each extra shot, as well as Angie's journaling, are matted on both sides of pink cardstock. The removable cards are kept secured in the envelope with an attractive ribbon-tied closure. Angie accented the envelope with a metal plaque treated with pink paint.

Using an envelope template, trace shape onto patterned vellum. Cut out and score according to manufacturer instructions.

Adhere punched squares for closure at each end. Set eyelets over squares.

Thread ribbon through each eyelet and knot.

Supplies: Patterned papers (K & Company, Memories Complete, National Cardstock); letter stickers (C-Thru Ruler, Wordsworth); stickers (Bo-Bunny Press, Karen Foster Design); rub-ons (Li'l Davis Designs); mod blocks, tags, frames and labels (KI Memories); colored staples, mini brads (Making Memories); chalk ink; ribbon; pen

First Friends

Two engaging interactive elements were incorporated onto this page about two young friends. The first is a small booklet comprised of cropped photos mounted on both sides of inked cardstock. The left borders of the cardstock "pages" were made wider to accommodate the ribbon fastener and were scored and inked. The pages were layered atop one another and threaded with ribbon through two small punched holes. The booklet's cover "binding" was covered with a red inked cardstock strip before being secured with a ribbon bow. The second element is a pull-out cardstock journaling block that features a mini brad-adorned label. It is tucked beneath a photo mat that was adhered along three sides to form a pocket.

TIP: Angie's mod-inspired tab accents not only serve a functional purpose, but they provide a little added punch to her interactive journaling card and pocket. Play with different ways to add a little something extra to your pulls, tabs, handles and hinges with the array of product currently available.

Summertime

Vibrantly matted photos flip to reveal additional summertime shots adorned with ribbon photo corners. Angie mounted three photos to her page background before layering each with another matted photo. To create the flip elements, metal hinges were affixed to the fronts of the photos and to the background page with glue dots.

TRICK: To mute the look of metal on her hinged accents, Angie applied a thin application of green acrylic paint to each to create a weathered effect.

Supplies: Patterned papers, metal hinges, ribbon photo corners (Making Memories); "summertime" accent and quote (KI Memories); white cardstock; pen; acrylic paint

Namesake

To honor the grandmother for whom her daughter is named, Angie created this endearing layout which boasts two interactive elements. The first is the hinged photo mat that opens to reveal another photo, which was matted on cardstock and adhered to the page. The second is a journaling tag featuring Angie's handwriting tucked behind the secondary photo. The tag was accented with ink, a letter sticker and a ribbon-adorned eyelet.

TECHNIQUE: To create a hinged photo mat element, simply mat your photo on cardstock and allow for extra space along the left border to accommodate the hinges. Align the hinges and secure to the photo mat and background page.

Supplies: Patterned paper (Design Originals); collage papers (DMD); red background paper (Paper Loft); wood grain paper (Pebbles); brown chalk ink (Clearsnap); fabric ribbon (K & Company); letter stencil (My Mind's Eye); metal nameplate, hinges, buckle (Karen Foster Design); extreme eyelet (Creative Imaginations); letter stickers (Creative Imaginations, EK Success, Sticker Studio); alphabet stamps, leather photo corners (Making Memories); fabric strip; fabric ribbon; brads; acrylic paint; clothing labels

Genuine American Hero

This masculine, military-inspired page featuring Angie's son in his dad's army fatigues contains two interactive elements. The first is a tag booklet that uses a manufactured tag as a template to create additional "pages." Each was aged with distress ink, linked together with twill and accented with a metal letter and chain. The cover is embellished with a sticker and metal post that secures the booklet closed with an elastic band. The second element is a file folder aged with distress ink featuring a patriotic poem. Mounted inside is handwritten journaling on ledger paper.

TRICK: Utilize manufactured products as foundations for your interactive elements. Doing so saves time and creates opportunity to embellish accents to make them your own.

Supplies: Camouflage patterned paper (source unknown); faux textured cardstock (source unknown); ledger paper, brads, label holder, metal letter (Making Memories); chalk ink (Clearsnap); twill (Creek Bank Creations); rivets (Chatterbox); walnut ink, elastic band (7 Gypsies); tags (Avery); distress ink (Ranger); stickers (Sticker Studio); file folder (Autumn Leaves); metal post (Rusty Pickle); poem (www.twopeasinabucket.com); pen; green paper; transparency

Deanna Rose Farmstead

A windowed file folder element and pull-out journaling tag add interactive interest to this nature-inspired page. The photo-showcasing file accent was created using a template and was embellished with stickers, inked journaling and a decorative paper clip. An elastic tie anchored between two rivets serves as an artful means of keeping the element closed. Angie treated her journaling tag with brown chalk ink and punched two additional holes that were then adorned with knotted ribbons. Angie used a craft knife to cut a slit just wider than the tag beneath the photo mat, then added a scrap paper "pocket" to the back of the page to house the tag.

TRICK: While leaving one side of the focal photo mat un-adhered would have also created a pocket for housing the tag, Angie's strategy solves the problem of her focal photo becoming dislodged from its repeated removal. The slit in the paper and hidden pocket enable her to more securely mount the photo mat to her page, all the while allowing the tag to easily slip in and out.

Supplies: Patterned papers (Autumn Leaves, Bazzill, Bo-Bunny Press, National Cardstock); stickers, sticker tags (Pebbles); rivets (Chatterbox); elastic tie (7 Gypsies); metal seal, antique conchos (K & Company); antique brads, straight pin, jump ring, metal letters (Making Memories); decorative paper clip (EK Success); tag (Avery); chalk ink (Clearsnap); ribbon

The Wieney Sisters

For this page celebrating a boy and his dogs, Angie created a booklet that contains three additional photos and journaling. To create her clever accent, Angie matted her extra photos in identical size, leaving a wider border at the top of each to accommodate the binding elements. She then embellished the "cover" with patterned paper and a blue molding strip and bound the pages together using scrapbook nails. To finish, Angie scored the mats just under the molding strip and added a title accent suspended by fibers.

TECHNIQUE: Here Angie proves that you can add interactive elements to your pages without adding a lot of bulk. Collect and showcase extra photos in a compact fashion with simple mats and binding.

Supplies: Patterned papers, scrapbook nails (Chatterbox); tag (Keller's Creations); conchos (Scrapworks); dimensional adhesive (JudiKins); Scrabble tile alphabet stickers, metal molding strip, safety pins, washer words, metal letter, rub-on words (Making Memories); alphabet stamps (Hero Arts); mini tag stickers (Pebbles); quote (www.twopeasinabucket.com); ink; ribbons; fibers

Charming

Although Angie's pocket and file folder element looks time-consuming to create, it is actually comprised of premade product that Angie embellished. To dress up the pocket and file folders, Angie inked the edges with brown ink and added letter stickers and journaling. She layered the pocket front with an inked tag, bead chain and patterned paper elements to create additional visual interest and dimension.

TIP: Easily personalize pre-made interactive elements by altering them with inks, chalks and other creative additions.

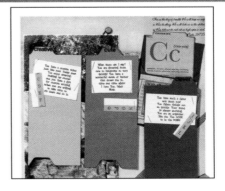

Supplies: Scrabble tile patterned paper (Design Originals); text patterned paper (7 Gypsies); pocket with file folders (Creek Bank Creations); chalk ink (Chatterbox); tag (Magic Scraps); "Charming" file tag (Autumn Leaves); paper clip (EK Success); ribbon charm, staples, bead chain (Making Memories); transparency; brown chalk; tan cardstock; ribbon

bloom

freshness

life

rebirth

splendor

spring is my favourite time of year. There is something so magical about the dead of winter suddenly coming alive again in vibrant colours and fresh green leaves. For me, the heart of springtime is captured in the blossoming trees, the explosions of pinks, purples, whites and yellows. The smells that waft over you from the lilacs and crabapples as you walk down the road. The transformation of bare wood into a celebration of rebirth. I can be doing something as mundane as running errands, and the sight of spring trees in full bloom will make my spirit soar and change my ordinary day into an extraordinary one. In my heart, this is truly ...

The Essence of Spring

Michelle
PESCE

CREATIVE TYPOGRAPHY

Michelle learned early the value of preserving family life in scrapbook albums. Thanks to the example instilled by her mother, Michelle can reflect back on scrapbooks she created throughout her entire adolescence and into college. Having happened upon "modern" scrapbooking eight years ago while browsing a hobby store, Michelle was once again inspired to chronicle special memories created as an adult within her own family.

To provide her loved ones with both memory-rich pages and an extension of herself, Michelle journals and creates title treatments using her own hand lettering and alphabet designs. Trained in calligraphy, Michelle notes her love for adding unique flourishes to letters and selecting just-right fonts naturally crossed over into her scrapbooking. "Whether I hand letter or do a title on the computer, it gives me so much creative control and I can really emphasize the theme and mood of my page by the writing style or font that I use." Michelle emphasizes that it is the one-of-a-kind quality of handwriting, not the appearance of it, that matters most. "The handwriting of the people I love is so entrenched in my heart and mind's eye for a zillion little reasons. Seeing it in whatever context can bring up a wellspring of emotion. A page with your sloping, less-than-perfect handwriting will mean so much more to your children than a perfect but sterile page that lacks any personal touches."

When not scrapbooking, Michelle is at work as a professional photographer and member of the board of directors of a theatre company she helped found. Additionally, she is wife to Tim and full-time mom to daughters Anneliese and Chiara in Arvada, Colorado.

Wedding Party

Michelle chose a script typeface for her handcut title to emphasize the formality and sophistication of her wedding portrait. By applying her own handwriting to vellum, Michelle added a purely personal element to the page to emphasize the significance of the day in her life. Michelle first typed and printed out the text on her computer to gauge how it would fit the allotted space, allowing room to accommodate a small collage comprised of a skeleton leaf, photo, die cut and tag.

Photos: Eliot Khuener Photography, Berkeley, California

TECHNIQUE: To achieve her handcut title, Michelle first printed the words onto scratch paper and temporarily adhered them to a piece of black cardstock. She then cut the words with a craft knife, removed the scratch paper template and adhesive and mounted the title to her layout.

Supplies: Gold webbing spray and leafing pen (Krylon); heart die cut (source unknown); skeleton leaves (All Night Media); burgundy and forest green cardstocks; fibers; pen; ribbon

Preparation of a Groom

A groom's page was kept fun and masculine with a mixture of typefaces. To add emphasis and dimension to "groom," Michelle coated letter stickers with Glossy Accents lacquer. Once dry, the letters were applied to metal-rimmed tags for an industrial look. Silver and circle-shaped black-and-white letter stickers provide an appealing contrast in style. Michelle simplified her own handwriting to complement the straight character of the other typefaces in her journaling block.

Photos: Cheryl Pesce, Trabuco Canyon, California

TRICK: To apply letter stickers with precision, arrange them on the edge of a clear ruler, position the ruler over your paper, then adhere the stickers to the paper by pulling the ruler out from underneath.

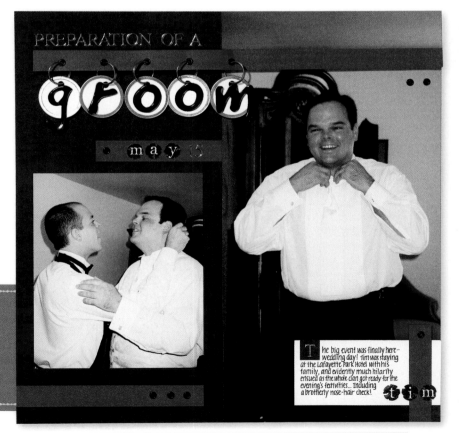

Supplies: Metal-rimmed tags (Avery); die-cut letters (Current); glossy lacquer (Ranger); letter stickers (Chatterbox, Pioneer); black and burgundy cardstocks; pen; foam adhesive; eyelets

Program

Michelle created her elegant handcut title from a computer font and perched it above her handwritten journaling block, allowing the "g" to hang over the edge for dimension. Using a light box and lined paper guide, Michelle journaled onto the same paper used in her wedding programs, making sure to accommodate a small cropped photo, printed ribbon and heart accent for added visual interest.

TIP: Incorporate textual elements from memorabilia as Michelle did here. The translucent first page of her wedding program provided the main portion of the pocket that holds her actual wedding program.

Supplies: Patterned papers (Making Memories, Mustard Moon); patterned cardstock (Neenah Paper); heart die cut (Sizzix); metal hearts, printed ribbon (Making Memories); gold leafing pen (Krylon); brads; chalk

Man of Letters

Michelle strategically used various typography treatments to correspond with a heritage photo of her grandfather, a former university president. Antique typewriter keys and a typewriter-style font carried the academic theme into the title and vellum-printed journaling block. Michelle handwrote "of" on scrap paper aged with chalk. Scrabble-style letters were created for the remainder of the title, while education-themed accents and an eyelet word combine for an appealing collage element.

TECHNIQUE: Michelle created her antique typewriter keys by fitting conchos with punched cardstock mounted with letter stickers and coated with clear dimensional lacquer. The Scrabble tiles were made from punched and chalked wood veneer paper mounted with letter stickers. Number values were added with pen and each tile was coated with lacquer. Both the keys and tiles were mounted with foam adhesive for dimension.

Supplies: Patterned papers (Design Originals); patterned cardstock (Mustard Moon); photo corners (Canson); wood veneer paper (Paper Adventures); metal-rimmed tag (Avery); copper foil tape (Hobby Lobby); mesh (Magic Mesh); swirl clip (www.work.org); printed transparencies (ArtChix); eyelet word (Making Memories); charm (Stampington & Company); letter stickers (Pioneer); conchos (Scrapworks); crystal lacquer (Sakura Hobby Craft); metallic rub-ons (Craf-T); stamp (Rubber Baby Buggy Bumpers); chalk; embossing powder; ink; embroidery floss; buttons; eyelets; fibers; foam adhesive; star brad

The Prettiest Pumpkin

Several typography details combine to add to the charm of this autumn-inspired layout. Michelle first chose a script font for "pumpkin," which was reverse-printed in a word processing program onto the back of patterned paper, cut with a craft knife and mounted beneath the focal photo. She used the same font for the main words of the title, which were embossed with clear powder immediately after being printed onto vellum. Michelle then added a straight, simplified version of her handwriting to add the remaining letters, cropped the title block and mounted it over a dimensional sticker.

TRICK: Michelle composed her journaling with a right-justified margin by first writing the lines on a scratch piece of paper. She then aligned the end of the line with her right-hand margin to determine where she needed to start writing the beginning of her lines, making adjustments as she went to keep the text even.

Supplies: Patterned paper (Amscan); dimensional pumpkin stickers (EK Success); brown cardstock; vellum; wire; chalks; eyelets; embossing powder; foam adhesives

Santa Fe

To emphasize her southwestern page theme, Michelle chose a rustic font for her dimensional title treatment. She reverse-printed the words onto the back of clay-colored cardstock and then cut each out with a craft knife. Since her cardstock journaling block was too thick to use with a light box, Michelle created small evenly spaced tick marks down each side and wrote the lines using a folded piece of cardstock to keep them straight. Once a full line of text was written, any missing "tails" of letters were then added.

TECHNIQUE: To create the look of cracked pottery in her title treatment, Michelle embossed the letters with several coats of extra thick embossing powder, adding new layers while the previous was still warm. Each letter was then bent while cooling to create the fragmented appearance, then allowed to set.

Supplies: Patterned paper (Amscan); metallic rub-ons (Craf-T); slide mounts (MOTOPhoto); sun buttons (JHB International); clay-colored cardstock; extra thick embossing powder; embossing ink; chalks; brads; decoupage adhesive; pen

Baby Expressions

This vibrant page is an example of how the "only two or three fonts per layout" rule can be broken to work to the design's advantage. Michelle successfully incorporated several fonts, including those represented in cropped portions of a printed transparency and a reverse-printed handcut title. She used a simplified version of her handwriting for contrast to complete both the title and journaling block.

TIP: If you plan to incorporate embellishments into your journaling block, trace a sketch of the element onto your paper prior to journaling to be sure your text will accommodate it.

Supplies: Patterned paper (Provo Craft); printed transparency (Creative Imaginations); rhinestone nailheads (Hirschberg Schutz & Co.); wire animal clips (Pier 1 Imports); blue cardstock; pen; ink; foam adhesive

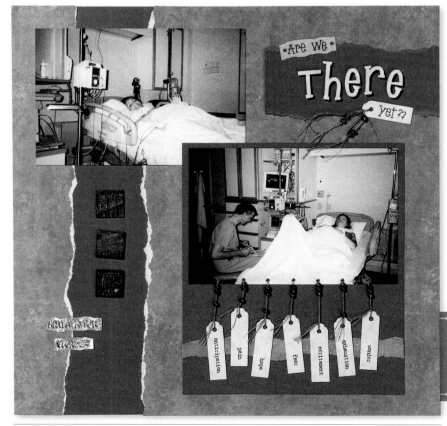

Are We There Yet?

Michelle chose a slightly irregular typeface for her title to reflect the anxiety and anticipation experienced while in labor. To give added emphasis to "there," she cut the letters out, added chalk detail and mounted them using foam adhesive. "Are we" was written onto vellum and torn, while "yet" was written on a chalked tag. Additional journaling tags were created by printing the words onto cardstock and cutting them into tags using a pattern. The words "anticipation" and "wonder" were embossed onto metal using a plain, all capital version of Michelle's handwriting for legibility.

TRICK: By using the same font for the entire title, Michelle created a unified look although she used different treatments for the different words.

Supplies: Patterned paper (Provo Craft); mosaic tiles (Mosaic Mercantile); metal (AMACO); beads (Westrim); mini eyelets (Creative Impressions); blue cardstock; vellum; embroidery floss; pen; chalk; foam adhesive

TRICK: Easily dress up letter stickers with products like die cuts, tiny frames, small tags, acrylic baubles and conchos for instant impact.

Supplies: Patterned papers (Design Originals); patterned vellum (Family Archives); metal frames (Making Memories); charms (Magic Scraps); conchos (Scrapworks); printed transparencies (ArtChix); letter stickers (EK Success); metallic rub-ons (Craf-T); punches (Emagination Crafts, Family Treasures); vellum; burgundy cardstock; ribbon; lace; eyelets; brads; buttons; silk flowers; pen; chalk; foam adhesive

Lors Show

In keeping with her Victorian page theme, Michelle created attractive concho letters reminiscent of the cameos so popular during that era from punched patterned paper, transparencies and letter stickers. The second portion of her title is comprised of letter stickers over patterned vellum. Her calligraphic journaling style provided a perfect fit for the page theme when applied to aged patterned paper beneath a metal frame.

Cut or punch portions of printed transparency to fit concho.

Cut or punch same size shape from desired background paper.

Layer transparency element over paper element, add letter sticker and place into concho. Bend the prongs down with your fingers or a hammer to hold in place.

A Walk in the Fall

Michelle first selected the distinctive, willowy font used for "Fall" to give it special emphasis and to influence the other typographical choices of this rich layout. To create contrast in the remainder of the title, a straight and more traditional font reminiscent of that of the "Wildlife Habitat" sign was used. This same typeface was repeated for the transparency-printed journaling block to create unity and balance.

Supplies: Patterned papers (Club Scrap, Scrap Ease); velvet leaves (Stampington & Co.); metallic rub-ons (Craf-T); parchment paper; forest green and burgundy cardstocks; transparency; burlap; acrylic paint; chalk; foam spacers

TECHNIQUE: Michelle created her overlapping, two-color title using Adobe Photoshop software, which was then printed onto parchment paper. Experiment with overlapping text elements to add drama and energy to your layout.

Precious

Favorite photos of Michelle's daughter were detailed with minimal and subdued typographical treatments to allow the photos to shine. To mimic the look of a dictionary definition, Michelle employed a straight and simplified version of her handwriting which was applied to vellum using a lined guide. The same technique was used to write additional detail onto metal-rimmed tags.

Supplies: Patterned papers (Hot Off The Press); flower snaps, punched tin squares, metal word (Making Memories); flower trim (www.GreenPear.com); metal-rimmed tags (Avery); silk ribbon; silk flowers and leaves; pen; foam adhesive; vellum; eyelets; embroidery floss; black cardstock; fabric

TIP: Vary handwritten words for added emphasis and to expand your writing style. Make simple changes by writing at a slant, playing with the spacing between letters, or by making your letters taller, shorter, thicker or thinner than you ordinarily would for a dramatic new look reflective of your page theme.

Spice Island Diving

Here a photo that said it all provided just-the-right title treatment for Michelle's shoreside layout. Her signature handwritten journaling is represented on a decorative block adorned with a watermark stamp, seashells and a mix of tiny glass marbles and real sand. Brads and bradwear form the word "Grenada," providing a formal contrast to the casual lettering of the main title and an eye-appealing inverse of the black letters on a white background shown in the photo.

Supplies: Patterned paper, rubber stamps, stencil, tiny glass marbles (Club Scrap); solvent and watermark inks (Tsukineko); coastal netting (Wal-Mart); mica (USArtQuest); sand dollars (Magic Scraps); metal-rimmed tag (Making Memories); seashells, sand and starfish (Bag of Beach); light blue, light green and tan cardstocks; pen; ink; embossing powder; fibers; chalk

TECHNIQUE: The bradwear letters were applied by rub-on transfer to the tops of silver brads, which were then inserted and secured to the background paper through pre-pierced holes.

lovin' summer

...some cups, and a bowl full of water!

Lovin' Summer

Michelle wanted a fun, carefree look for her title and journaling to accompany photos of her daughter enjoying simple pleasures on a sunny summer day. The font used for the title and subtitle was selected to look as though it was casually jotted down and was differentiated in weight and size for emphasis. Michelle printed her title onto self-adhesive transparency film and mounted it over a painted background.

TRICK: Keep your handwritten journaling straight and neat by slipping a lined guide beneath the vellum. Sets of calligraphy sheets in various sizes and line widths can be purchased at stationery shops. You can also create your own in a word processing program or by measuring and drawing dark lines on a sheet of white paper.

Supplies: Patterned papers (Club Scrap, Rocky Mountain Scrapbook Company); stamps (Hero Arts); paints (LuminArte); transparency (Grafix); ribbon (Me & My Big Ideas); foam adhesive; embossing powder; pen

Christmas Is a Time For...

To best suit these festive yuletide photos, Michelle kept her journaling to a minimum and instead found fun ways to showcase what few words are featured. She mimicked the style of her "Christmas" rub-on word using her own handwriting in a bulleted list accented with eyelets. Punched stars provide fun identification tags that feature names written in gold pen.

TIP: Make use of the vast variety of rub-on letters and words available, which may be applied to photos, papers and accents in a flash for instant and artsy typographical treatments.

Supplies: Patterned papers (Carolee's Creations, Provo Craft); printed ribbon, rub-on word (Making Memories); star charms (www.alltheextras.com); star punch (Carl); yellow cardstock; chalk; eyelets; embroidery floss; pen

Mom's Lessons in Motherhood

Since her layout is about lessons, Michelle chose to write her journaling and photo captions in a simplified version of her handwriting to make it appear like that of a student's. The typeface for "Motherhood" was selected because it offered enough contrast from Michelle's handwriting, had a feminine feel and adequately filled the designated space. A larger version of Michelle's handwriting provides the first portion of the title.

TIP: Easily dress up journaling blocks and captions with freehand borders like those Michelle incorporated here, breaking the lines to accommodate the ascenders and descenders of the letters.

Supplies: Patterned paper (Anna Griffin, Creative Imaginations); ribbon photo corners (Anna Griffin); letter stickers (Creative Imaginations); metal charm (Magenta); crystal lacquer (Sakura Hobby Craft); vellum; ribbon; tiny glass marbles

Little Fingers Little Toes

For an especially meaningful touch, Michelle incorporated the hand-, foot- and fingerprints of her newborn daughter to comprise her title and subtitle treatments. Michelle designed the title font to look "childish" and penned each letter at a slant to evoke a sense of movement. Baby Anna's fingerprints were used to form the word "Baby" on the journaling block. Rub-on words, each in a different font, are unified in their color and placement on the photos.

TRICK: Rather than struggle to get descent and precise original hand- and footprints on her title block, Michelle scanned the best of each into her computer, customized their placement and handwrote her lettering on top of the prints.

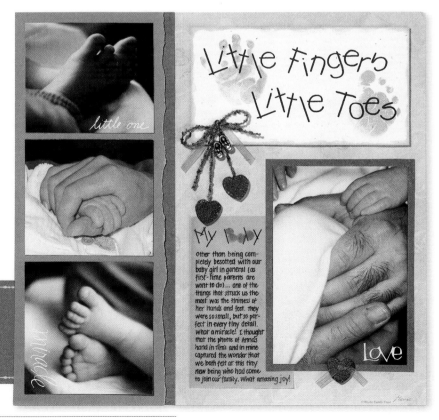

Supplies: Patterned paper (Frances Meyer); rub-on words (Making Memories); vellum; wooden hearts; baby charm; stamping ink; embossing powder; fibers; eyelet; foam adhesive; ribbon; pen

Denise TUCKER

TEXTURE

In 1997, Denise opted out of a crop party in order to apply the ten dollars required for attendance to scrapbook supplies she saw advertised at a local store. It was this practical choice, in addition to discovering scrapbooking publications, that prompted Denise to explore scrapbooking on her own terms as a potential hobby. Seven years later and her initial thriftiness since thwarted, Denise is a constant cropper whose supplies span a vast and varied spectrum.

Denise says that her acceptance of having elements on her pages that are not necessarily acid- and lignin-free have kept her open to trying "new and lumpy products." She notes, "The artistic aspect of this hobby is what I find most appealing, so I gradually began incorporating more and more varied textures onto my pages." Consequently, Denise's willingness to experiment with and feature interesting product evolved into her highly tactile signature style. For Denise, devising the methodology for building her pages is as rewarding as the final product. "The hands-on process of scrapbooking is as important to me as the end result. I don't worry about spending hours on a layout. I'm not in a race to scrapbook all of my photos. I just want to enjoy the progression of scrapbooking some of my favorites."

In addition to her scrapbooking, Denise works as a junior high school special education teacher. She lives in Versailles, Indiana, with husband Trace and their four children, sons Trent, Tanner, Ty and daughter Toria.

Toria's Friends

The dramatic texture of paint-treated embossed paper was accented with several other dimensional items. Denise created her bold title using a stencil and stencil paste. A vellum photo mat was embossed for additional detail, while ribbon, acrylic labels and metal brads represent a variety of other textures.

TRICK: Add instant texture to any layout with embossed paper. Applying rub-ons, paint or ink to their surfaces is an easy and striking way to emphasize interesting patterns.

Supplies: Embossed paper (Provo Craft); patterned paper (Karen Foster Design); dimensional paint, stencil (Delta); acrylic labels (Paperbilities); labels (Dymo); rub-ons (Making Memories); ribbon (Me & My Big Ideas, Offray); vellum; brads; eyelet; acrylic paint; ink; foam adhesive

Shells

Lush texture complements a striking photo of Denise's daughter exploring along the seashore. The unique background was created using a rubber stamp and household iron to heat emboss velvet. Cheesecloth elements, an assortment of shells and paint-altered metal molding pull in additional texture and sea-inspired detail.

TECHNIQUE: Emboss velvet by placing rubber stamps rubber-side-up on an ironing board and covering with velvet, nap-side-down against the stamp. Spritz the back of the velvet with water and press iron set on "cotton" setting onto velvet over stamp. Hold in place for approximately 10-15 seconds and lift to reveal the permanently impressed image.

Supplies: Stamps (Hot Potatoes, PSX Design); metal molding (Making Memories); metallic rub-ons (Craft-T) cheesecloth (Prym-Dritz); shells (U.S. Shell); velvet; acrylic paint; foam adhesive

Treasures at Sea

Denise mimicked the look and feel of sand on her page by applying Make It Stone! paint to a foam core board background. Once thoroughly dry, Denise treated the surface with shades of brown metallic rub-ons. She then applied several hues of blue and turquoise inks directly to the foam core board and embossed them with extra thick embossing powder, repeating the process two more times. Cheesecloth, coastal netting, shells and a foam paper-cut title provide additional eye-catching dimension.

TRICK: To achieve the look of sanded photo edges in half the time, apply acrylic paint with a dry brush along the borders for an artful touch.

Supplies: Foam board (Hunt Corp.); foam paper (Darice); printed transparencies (Design Originals); textured paint, gold leaf pen, white paint pen (Krylon); rubber stamps (Stamp Craft); rub-ons (Making Memories); label holders (Creative Imaginations, Making Memories); shells, coastal netting (U.S. Shell); metallic rub-ons (Craf-T); acrylic paint; ink; extra thick embossing powder; brads; cheesecloth

Pure

Plush white velvet mounted over blue cardstock created a soft, subtle background for additional textural details. The title was created by embossing the velvet background with rubber stamps and is accented with a paint-treated decorative stick pin. Wooden letters and watch crystals add depth while stamped twill, ribbon, sheer netting and painted eyelets lend additional visual interest.

Photos: FoxFish Photography, Arvada, Colorado

TECHNIQUE: Denise applied white paint and embossing powder to achieve the supple, somewhat "wet" appearance of her wooden letters.

Supplies: Rubber stamps (Ma Vinci's Reliquary, Stamp Craft); wooden letters, decoupage adhesive (Plaid); twill (Creek Bank Creations); ribbon charms, decorative brads, mini eyelets (Making Memories); metal corner (Eggery Place); stick pin (EK Success); watch crystals (Deluxe Plastic Arts); metallic rubs (Craf-T); sheer netting; ribbon foam adhesive; acrylic paint; ink; embossing powder

Six Going On 16

This boyish and rugged layout boasts several textures, both dimensional and faux. A burgundy faux-wood background matted on cardstock is layered with strips of denim-patterned paper, wood and woven patterned papers. Denise matted the photos on cardboard and duct tape patterned paper and mounted each with foam adhesive. A journaling tag comprised of wood patterned paper and embossed journaling pulls out from beneath the bottom photo and is tied with a strip of bandanna material. Dimensional textures include inked aida cloth, acrylic paint-treated wood letters and crackle finish metal brads.

TIP: When you want the look of several textures but don't feel comfortable adding the items to your page, look to faux textured elements without compromising on eye-appeal.

Supplies: *Patterned paper (Flair Designs, Karen Foster Design, Pebbles); wooden letters (Plaid); star brads (Magic Scraps); decorative washer (EK Success); crackle paint (Delta); aida cloth (Charles Craft); stamps (Stamp Craft); metallic rub-ons (Craf-T); transparency; acrylic paint; embossing powder; foam adhesive*

Boys of Summer

This all-American page artfully captures Denise's boys' favorite pastime. Stitched and paint-treated canvas was mounted on a black cardstock background with spray adhesive and bordered with buttonhole strips. Wet, crumpled and ironed papers were coated with a layer of decoupage adhesive to assume the look of leather and were mounted with foam adhesive. Metal letters, brads and charms incorporate smooth texture and dimension while leather stitches mimic a baseball mitt.

TECHNIQUE: The rustic finish on the star brads was achieved by coating each with crackle medium. Before drying completely, a layer of yellow acrylic paint was applied, forming cracks in the direction of the brush strokes. Once dry, a tea varnish was added for an aged effect.

Supplies: *Patterned paper (Karen Foster Design); button loop borders (Sweetwater); metal letters (K & Company, Making Memories, Provo Craft); letter rub-ons, number stamps (Making Memories); star brads (Magic Scraps); dog tag and chain (SWIBCO); charms (Beadery); leather laces (Designer's Library); crackle paint, tea stain varnish (Delta); decoupage adhesive (Plaid); thread; foam adhesive*

Freedom

Denise created a patriotic layout with old Americana charm. The aged look of the background patterned papers was accomplished by misting each with water, crumpling, ironing and highlighting the creases with white ink and brown metallic rubs. Metal accents were distressed by painting with white pen and sponging with red acrylic paint and brown metallic rubs. Cut foam paper letters mounted over aged ribbon add dimension while lace trim and bows provide feminine touches.

TRICK: To give her foam paper letters a childlike quality, Denise coated letter stamps with an uneven application of red acrylic paint.

Supplies: Patterned papers (Flair Designs, Karen Foster Design, Rusty Pickle); foam paper (Darice); label holder (Creative Imaginations); star brads (Magic Scraps); metal letters (K & Company); metal corner (Eggery Place); metallic rub-ons (Craf-T); stamps (Ma Vinci's Reliquary); sticker (Karen Foster Design); vellum; various ribbon; lace trim; mini brads; paint pen; acrylic paint; ink; decoupage adhesive; embroidery floss; foam adhesive

Allergy Testing

By applying a light application of black paint to red fabric, Denise accentuated the texture and re-created the look of the shirt her son is wearing in the photo. Transparency-printed journaling was embossed and layered over corrugated cardboard that had been spackled with embossing paste. Molding strips were shaded with metallic rubs and coated with decoupage adhesive for sheen. The woven look of the focal photo mat was highlighted with acrylic paint. Labels and a syringe add additional tactile elements.

TRICK: Denise easily added a subtle layer to her layout by mounting her focal photo over a file folder accent.

Supplies: Molding strips (Chatterbox); file folder (DMD); labels (Dymo); dimensional paint (Delta); metallic rub-ons (Craf-T); watch crystal (Deluxe Plastic Arts); stamps (Ma Vinci's Reliquary); fabric; brads; acrylic paint; decoupage adhesive; transparency; embossing powder; ink; foam adhesive; cardboard; syringe; business card

TRICK: Denise altered her metal animal charms to better fit the colors used in her page by painting them with a silver paint pen.

Soft hands, with a chipped manicure, gently cradled a found treasure. Yes, Toria has always had a special place in her heart for all of God's creatures. She was thoroughly entertained as she played with this little toad during the Sunday school picnic. I wonder if she realizes that we consider her one of God's most precious creations. May 2004

Supplies: *Embossed paper (Provo Craft); ribbon charm, letter rub-ons (Making Memories); paint pen (Krylon); charms (Boutique Trims); tin lid frame (Lee Valley); cork circles (Parker Metal Corp.); extra thick embossing powder; foam adhesive*

All God's Creatures

Little Toria's enchantment with a toad is endearingly captured on this highly tactile page. Denise cleverly altered textured background paper to take on a "reptilian" appearance by enhancing it with paint, ink and decoupage adhesive. Shiny texture was introduced through transparency-printed embossed journaling, a tin lid frame accent and animal charms. Various ribbons and a title comprised of paint pen-treated cork letters and a foam adhesive-mounted word round out the design.

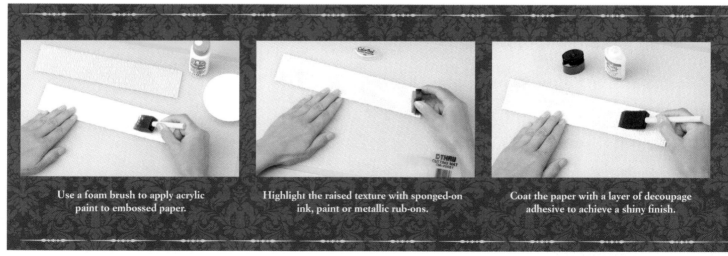

Use a foam brush to apply acrylic paint to embossed paper.

Highlight the raised texture with sponged-on ink, paint or metallic rub-ons.

Coat the paper with a layer of decoupage adhesive to achieve a shiny finish.

Christmas 2003

Denise wrapped up this Christmastime layout with several symbolic touches, all the while incorporating her trademark texture. Areas of the embossed background paper were shaded with ink to represent the look of wrapping paper. Ribbon charms were painted with a gold leafing pen and strung on ribbons to enhance the package theme and take on the look of tree ornaments. The texture of the cardstock holiday card accent was highlighted with metallic rubs, while a glossy vellum envelope with gold edging adds additional sheen.

Supplies: Patterned paper (source unknown); textured cardstock, ribbon charms (Making Memories); glassine envelope (Impress Rubber Stamps); decorative corner (Eggery Place); discs (Rollabind); gold foil pen (Krylon); metallic rubs (Craf-T); ribbon; ink; decoupage adhesive; foam adhesive

TECHNIQUE: Re-create Denise's dimensional "2003" accents by printing the year, cutting each number out and placing it inside a Rollabind disc. Fill the discs with decoupage adhesive for a sealant and to add shine.

All That I Am...

Denise created the highly tactile background for her tribute page using an attractive paper technique. She applied spray adhesive to cut and torn sections of patterned paper and layered each piece with crumpled white tissue paper. Denise then flattened the tissue paper to allow wrinkles to form, then applied metallic rub-ons and a coating of decoupage adhesive. Once dry, the pieces were mounted to the page. Twill, lace, stamped mica and notions provide additional texture.

Supplies: Patterned papers (Making Memories); stick pin, decorative washers, vellum postcard sticker (EK Success); rubber stamps (PSX Design, Stamp Craft); transparency; twill; tissue paper; lace trim; ink; acrylic paint; mica; embossing powder; embroidery floss; foam adhesive; decoupage adhesive; antique buttons

TIP: Select page additions for symbolic, not just ornamental, reasons. Here Denise incorporated letter closures and a postcard element to honor her father's love for letter writing, and rose-patterned paper, a hat pin and antique buttons to represent some of her mother's favorites.

Six

Embossed papers altered with ink and paint assume the look of birthday cake icing in this festive layout. A foam core board background was sprayed with Make It Stone! textured paint, allowed to dry, then treated with white acrylic paint. Embossed papers were given a light "frosting" of white acrylic paint, as were the textured cardstock journaling block and photo mat. For her title, Denise mounted painted letter brads over a small section of aida cloth to bring in additional texture.

Supplies: Embossed paper, letter brads (Provo Craft); textured cardstock (Bazzill); textured paint, stained-glass paint (Krylon); mini brads, metal-rimmed tags (Making Memories); stickers (Pebbles); aida cloth (Charles Craft); foam core board; ink

TECHNIQUE: Denise achieved the look of air brushed cake icing by spraying white embossed paper with green stained-glass paint.

Pure Girl

This lovely layout featuring floral elements, ribbon and hints of glitter exudes girlish femininity. A floral embossed paper background provided immediate texture and took on a sheen once layered with a printed transparency. "Toria" and "2004" were given additional impact with foam adhesive and epoxy stickers. To customize her premade dimensional floral accents and border, Denise further enhanced them with glitter spray and decoupage adhesive.

TRICK: Create the look of premade dimensional floral accents by layering cut floral elements from patterned paper over patterned paper of the same design. Mount with foam adhesive and enhance with glitter, crystal lacquer or decoupage adhesive for custom, cost-efficient embellishments.

Supplies: *Embossed paper (Provo Craft); printed transparency (Artistic Expressions); die cuts and border (K & Company); letter rub-ons (Making Memories); epoxy tiles (EK Success); glitter spray (Krylon); metallic rub-ons (Craf-T); ribbon; brads; acrylic paint; decoupage adhesive; ink; foam adhesive*

Tilly

Twill, wood, metal and acrylic textures are all elements Denise used to celebrate her faithful companion, Tilly. The vintage-style patterned papers were misted, crumpled and ironed, then layered with strips of inked patterned paper. Stamped twill accents the focal photo and cut pieces are used to highlight each epoxy page corner. Label holders, woven labels and brads create a visual triangle while stacked wooden letters comprise the dimensional title.

TECHNIQUE: Brown metallic rubs and black Rub 'n Buff were used to colorize the wood letters before being stacked in offset fashion.

Supplies: *Patterned papers (Design Originals); wooden letters (Plaid); twill (Creek Bank Creations); label holders (Making Memories); acrylic corners (EK Success); woven label (Me & My Big Ideas); letter stamps (PSX Design, Stamp Craft); metallic rub-ons (Craft-T); pigment powder (AMACO); brads; ink; foam adhesive*

Remember

To capture her son's growth, Denise chose under-stated accents and faux textures to keep the page masculine. Leather paper was treated with acrylic paint to emphasize its texture. Metal watch face label holders accent faux ribbon and belt stickers. For her tag accent and title, Denise used faux stone paper treated with black ink. Three foam adhesive-mounted strips provide depth and frame embossed journaling, while a ribbon-threaded decorative washer pulls in additional texture for a finishing touch.

TIP: Adding dimensional accents to faux-textured stickers creates a convincing alternative for the real thing, but without adding a lot of bulk.

Supplies: Leather paper (Freckle Press); patterned paper (Westrim); label holders, decorative washer (EK Success); buckle sticker (Memories Complete); transparency; ribbon; acrylic paint; ink; embossing ink; foam adhesive

TLT

Both "touchable" and faux textures help to create the outdoorsy feel of this layout. Faux wood-patterned papers comprise the page background, which was then layered with matted and foam-adhesive-mounted photos. Journaling printed on frayed aida cloth was shaded with metallic rub-ons, layered with a metal nameplate and mounted with foam adhesive. Letter and word stickers mounted with foam adhesive and framed with label holders complete the design.

TRICK: To give her faux-wood background a more realistic look, Denise cut strips of several wood-grained papers into strips, inked their edges and mounted them one atop the other on black cardstock to look like planks.

Supplies: Patterned papers (Karen Foster Design); cross-stitch material (Charles Craft); label holders (Making Memories); letter tags, stickers (Pebbles); metallic rub-ons (Craf-T); acrylic paint; brads; ink; foam adhesive

Andrea Lyn VETTEN-MARLEY

SEWING AND NOTIONS

Andrea can trace her scrapbooking origins back to when she was 12 years old, when her love for saving memorabilia and taking photos inspired her to creatively combine the two in albums. This early experience, in addition to sewing skills acquired at a young age, would ultimately pave the way for Andrea's modern scrapbook projects and the development of her signature style.

For Andrea, incorporating sewing and notions into her layouts is second nature. "Using fabric, machine and hand stitching and notions comes very naturally for me. It's simply a medium of expression, like painting might be for someone else." Andrea also appreciates the artistic possibilities and challenges her signature style provides. "Using fabrics and notions opens up a whole new world of design and textures for scrapbook layouts, cards and other projects. It's an enjoyable challenge to create new uses for ordinary notions like snaps or hook-and-eye closures." Though tactile fabrics and intricate stitches adorn her pages, Andrea often looks to various media advertisements for design inspiration. Striving to continuously tap into her self-described "mad scientist" mentality, Andrea notes, "My appetite to create and learn new techniques is insatiable. The more I work creatively with scrapbooking and the more techniques I learn, the more I enjoy what I do."

In addition to scrapbooking, Andrea works as an assistant manager at a scrapbook store. She has two children, son Brandon and daughter Brianna, and lives in Aurora, Colorado.

Splish Splash

To keep her bathtime layout playful, Andrea chose cool "water colors" of blue and green and added fun aquatic-themed accents. Iron-on words make for a vibrant title treatment, while fish appliqués and tiny hand-sewn bead "bubbles" provide endearing added details. Blue rickrack and border stitching cleverly mimic the look of water ripples.

TIP: For adhering especially small beads to a page background, hand sewing provides a much cleaner look than would be achieved using a liquid adhesive.

Supplies: Patterned paper (Daisy D's); fish appliqués (source unknown); iron-on letters (SEI); pearl beads (Westrim); vellum (Club Scrap); rickrack

The Adventure of Being Caley

Andrea liked the color combination between these fabrics and cardstocks so much she opted to print her photos in black-and-white to avoid competition between the two. Two different machine stitches and intricate hand-sewn ribbon "paths" for dragonfly appliqués provide delicate detail. Hand-sewn tiny pearl beads provide added visual interest placed along the ribbon.

Photos: Patricia Senn, Aurora, Colorado

TECHNIQUE: To create her ribbon "paths," Andrea used super tape to secure the ends of the ribbon to the back of the page. She then tacked the ribbon in place with a simple stitch at each of several pre-pierced holes, adding a bead each time she came back through the hole from the back, securing the bead and ribbon together.

Supplies: Sea foam, powder blue and light blue textured cardstocks (Bazzill); beads (Jesse James); dragonfly appliqués (Hirschberg Schutz & Co.); embroidery floss; sheer ribbon; floral fabric

Explore & Discover

Glistening buttons and beads, cool, tranquil hues and eye-catching crest shapes comprise this sea-inspired layout. Andrea crafted her bead border by first pre-piercing sets of holes at equal intervals around the page. She then used an "in and out" stitch to come up through the hole, pick up a series of beads, then back out the next hole, repeating until the design was complete. To create the wave crests, Andrea cut the shape from patterned paper, mounted the sheet over navy blue cardstock, and placed the cut-out crest in the upper right-hand corner. Each shape was accented with stitches between pre-pierced holes, a technique that was repeated at each photo corner as well.

Photos: Creative Images Photography, Huntsville, Alabama

TECHNIQUE: For the stitched and beaded crest shape, Andrea employed the same technique as on her page border, except no additional beads were added to the space between the pre-pierced holes.

Supplies: Textured sea foam cardstock (Bazzill); patterned paper (Magenta); beads (Jesse James); decorative brads, rub-on letters (Making Memories); navy blue cardstock, vellum; teal embroidery floss; vintage buttons

Sisters Are...

To complement sweet flower-adorned photos of two little ladies, Andrea created feminine floral designs in the corners of her layout using a template as a guide. Vine and leaf patterns were pre-pierced and stitched with green embroidery floss. The blossoms are comprised of silk flowers with bead centers.

Photos: Creative Images Photography, Huntsville, Alabama

TIP: Look to silk flowers to add instant dimension and a feminine element to pages, which can be affixed to pages with adhesive as well as with stitches. Removing the plastic backings will keep the flowers from adding bulk to the page.

Supplies: Patterned green and blue papers (Cloud 9 Design); embroidery template (Timeless Touches); beads (Jesse James); green embroidery floss; vellum; silk flowers

TRICK: Andrea's quilted page background looks especially authentic as a result of her choice in muted pattern papers featuring vintage and floral designs.

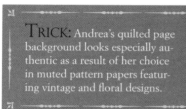

Supplies: Floral patterned paper (Daisy D's); children's patterned paper (Rusty Pickle); crochet ribbon (Wrights); crochet flowers, heart buttons (Jesse James); blue cardstock; embroidery floss; vellum

My dear sweet Ruby,
Being born in these modern times will make life easier for you in so many ways. You will have the very best your daddy and I can give you. That is why I make you this promise: You will be raised with an abundance of Old Fashioned Love and values that will truly support you in good times and bad for all of your life.
Love you forever,
Mommy

Old Fashioned Love

Old Fashioned Love

Look closely and you'll see the quilted look of this page was achieved by machine stitching assorted squares and rectangles from several patterned papers. The perfectly paired colors, prints and subtle stitching are so complementary that the background appears almost seamless. Additional machine sewing lends dimension to the triple-matted photo and double-matted title treatment, while crochet ribbon frames the page for added texture. Crochet flowers and hand-sewn buttons comprise the final details of this endearing composition.

Photo: Aaron Kafer, Ft. Lupton, Colorado

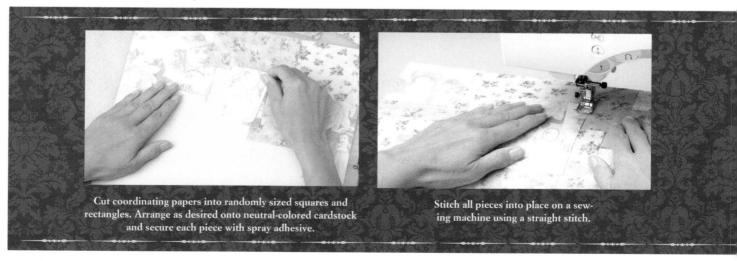

Cut coordinating papers into randomly sized squares and rectangles. Arrange as desired onto neutral-colored cardstock and secure each piece with spray adhesive.

Stitch all pieces into place on a sewing machine using a straight stitch.

Common Threads

In order to create a layout vintage in feel but without altering a precious family heirloom, Andrea used fabric from thrift store pillowcases to achieve an authentic look. She printed her photos and journaling onto fabric taken from the back of a pillowcase, frayed the ends and hand sewed each onto the portion of the pillowcase to be used for the page background. After adding lace, beads, ribbon and embroidery by hand, Andrea mounted the quilting on cardstock, securing it flat with tacky tape. Finally, machine stitches were incorporated throughout and alphabet stamps were applied directly to the fabric background with a solvent based ink.

Supplies: Butterfly and hummingbird beads (Hirschberg Shutz & Co.); alphabet stamps (Making Memories); ribbon (Making Memories, Me & My Big Ideas); quilted pillowcase; lace; pink embroidery floss; lace trim

TRICK: In addition to using super tape to adhere the fabric to the cardstock, Andrea added hand stitches at each corner to keep the material flush.

True Blue Love

Crisp stitching and several whimsical notions combine on this page commemorating a little sleeping beauty. Handmade fabric bows with snap centers, butterfly appliqués and heart buttons Andrea purchased twenty years ago for use on her own daughter's outfits add both personal and artistic touches. To carry over the "true blue" theme, Andrea incorporated blue fabric with a feminine pattern. For added interest, she frayed the edges of her fabric title and journaling blocks, which are made from fabric from baby clothes.

Photos: Jill Walker, Centennial, Colorado

Supplies: Textured navy and royal blue cardstocks (Bazzill); butterfly appliques (Hirschberg Schutz & Co.); heart buttons (source unknown); floral fabric; fabric from baby clothes; embroidery floss; snaps

TIP: Use acid-free spray adhesive to affix cardstock and/or fabric to a background before sewing them on to prevent ripples from developing.

Trust Is a Promise Kept

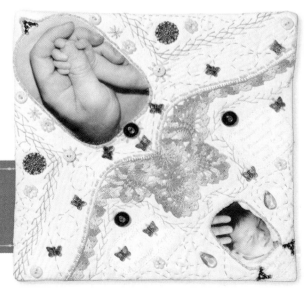

Employing the same technique as the previous layout, Andrea breathed fresh life into a thrift store find for this pillowy-soft layout. Before mounting the 13" cut pillowcase fabric, Andrea applied pieces of muslin and batting material of the same size to a piece of cardstock using spray adhesive. She then cut smaller pieces of fabric for printing the photos and journaling and affixed them to cardstock with spray adhesive. The pieces were then fed through a printer, trimmed and applied to the layout with spray adhesive. Decorative machine stitching and hand-sewn crochet lace, buttons, beadwork and metal elements were added throughout.

TIP: Incorporate material from jeans, quilt pieces, baby and children's clothes as well as vintage pieces that hold no sentimental value. Yard sales, flea markets, antique stores and even your own closets, basements and attics can yield a treasure-trove of finds perfect for a page.

Supplies: Pillowcase; blue and peach embroidery floss; buttons (Jesse James); beads; metal filigrees (source unknown); cardstock; batting; muslin

Colorado Cowboy

Essentially every element from a cowboy's closet found its place on this playful page. Rust patterned paper was hand-sewn to the brown background page at an askew angle through pierced holes. Suspender clasps and washer-adorned leather strips laced through eyelets dress up fabric photo mats. Double-mounted suede paper journaling blocks were strung with fibers and rivets accent each page corner.

Photos: Lifetouch/JC Penney, Aurora, Colorado

TRICK: By simply alternating between machine and hand-stitching, entirely different looks can be achieved between layouts or even on the same page.

Supplies: Rust patterned paper, rivets (Chatterbox); suede paper (Hot Off The Press); washer words (Making Memories); leather lacing (Tandy); suspender clasps (Prym-Dritz); embroidery floss; ribbon; black chalk ink; fibers; fabric scraps; eyelets

Charming Boyhood

Sometimes small, precise stitches are not what a page calls for. An endearing assemblage of spontaneous hand-stitching and whimsically strung fibers was just the right treatment for this layout of aged collaged elements. Andrea hand-sewed torn and chalked patterned paper to the background page with embroidery floss through randomly pierced holes. Buttons were attached by hand and fiber was strung between rivets at the corners of each photo mat. The torn title treatment was embellished with fibers strung through eyelets in a criss-cross pattern, in keeping with the worn, rustic page theme.

Photos: Lifetouch/JC Penney, Aurora, Colorado

TIP: When hand-stitching on layouts, pre-pierce holes to make it much easier for an average needle to pass through thicker papers such as cardstock.

Supplies: Plaid patterned paper, rivets (Chatterbox); definition paper (Carolee's Creations); faux textured patterned papers (Making Memories); extra thick embossing powder; embroidery floss; fibers; buttons; pin tips; various chalk inks

"Auntie Ann, Let's go for a walk in the garden!" Gillian, I treasure every moment I get to spend with you. Today you showed me all around Grandma Vetten's beautiful garden, pointing out each flower by name. The snapdragons were your favorite, and you took great pride showing me how they can open their mouths and talk. A lifetime ago, I was your age and my Mommy, your Grandma was showing me how the snapdragons talk. Isn't it wonderful how the sweet things in life repeat themselves!

Snapdragons

Gillian Athena Leah Vetten
Nearly 5 years old
June 11, 2004

Snapdragons

To achieve an earthy outdoors theme, Andrea chose natural-colored muslin to layer over her page background and muslin snap tape to cleverly complement her snapdragons theme. Red rickrack adorned with overall clasp slides add a touch of color and echoe Gillian's dress. Black-and-white gingham provides a touch of contrast and mimics the lattice fence in the photo background. Machine stitching and an iron-on title complete this crisp composition.

TECHNIQUE: Iron-ons are a quick solution for crisp-looking title and design elements. They peel off like stickers and dress up fabric and paper alike.

Supplies: Seed bag patterned paper (Rusty Pickle); iron-on (SEI); natural cardstock; muslin scrap; snap tape; rickrack; thread; gingham ribbon; buckles; overall clasp slides; distress ink

Ruth

A delicate lace border and doily provided perfect page additions for this heritage photo. Here Andrea layered lace trim beneath fabric-patterned paper that was stitched to a cardstock background. She then incorporated timeless elements such as photo corners and buttons with silk flowers placed along whimsical stitched vines. For an elegant touch, Andrea hand-stitched her page title.

TECHNIQUE: Andrea creatively added interest to a doily accent by threading thin ribbon through a portion of the design. This detail, in combination with a button center, provided an easy but elegant finishing touch.

Supplies: Fabric-patterned paper (Club Scrap); brown cardstock; lace trim; crocheted doily; silk flowers; beads; buttons; vellum; embroidery floss; photo corners; ribbon

Ruth

Of all the things you taught us, the most important was Love & Patience. You gave Love & Patience unselfishly to all those around you. Ruth, you will be dearly missed!

Ruth Gardner

TIP: Andrea's design works especially well since the pattern of the background fabric is made dimensional with the butterfly appliqué.

caley

I especially love this photo of you Caley. I carefully removed all the thorns from this rose so that you could enjoy its beauty without the pain of getting poked. How I wish I could remove all the thorns in life for you. Anything that hurts you, hurts me. I want you to experience all the beauty and joy of life and not have to also experience the pain. Life has already been a bit of a struggle for you, and you have made a remarkable recovery from your surgery. In reality, I know that in order to fully appreciate the joys in life, we all have to experience the pain as well. Still, it does not stop me in my desire as your mother to remove every thorn I am able to.

Supplies: Rub-on letters (source unknown); butterfly appliqué (Hirschberg Schutz & Co.); sheer fabric; sheer ribbon; gold and green embroidery floss; yellow vellum; dark and light green cardstocks

Caley

Sheer ribbon borders woven at their intersection artfully contain the sweet photo and design of this layout. Sheer patterned fabric was stitched to green cardstock before being stitched to the background and layered with ribbon. The "flight path" of the butterfly appliqué was highlighted with gold embroidery floss threaded through pierced holes to further draw the eye to the photo and journaling.

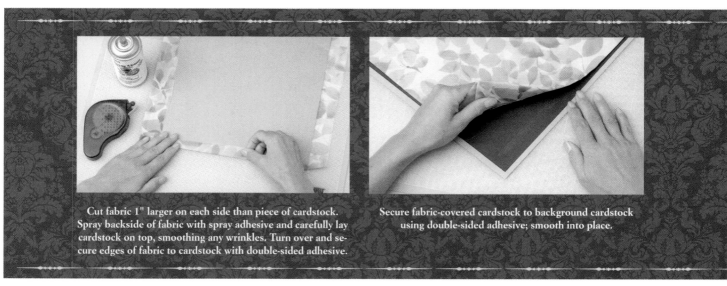

Cut fabric 1" larger on each side than piece of cardstock. Spray backside of fabric with spray adhesive and carefully lay cardstock on top, smoothing any wrinkles. Turn over and secure edges of fabric to cardstock with double-sided adhesive.

Secure fabric-covered cardstock to background cardstock using double-sided adhesive; smooth into place.

Susan

Delicate embroidering added an elegant touch to this feminine page. The patterned paper and photo mat were machine stitched while the whimsical vines and page title were created using a manufacturer pattern and computer font. Andrea pierced evenly spaced holes directly through each pattern and sewed them with embroidery floss using a back stitch. For the heart accents, Andrea again used an embroidery pattern, stitching according to specific design instructions. To dress up the page, Andrea added ribbon page corners and dimensional flower stickers.

TECHNIQUE: In addition to utilizing manufactured hand embroidery patterns, you can craft your own by printing or drawing on regular paper. Pierce holes in even intervals, sew with embroidery floss and you have a custom-created design.

Supplies: Textured light and dark green cardstocks (Bazzill); patterned paper, dimensional flower stickers (EK Success); ribbon corners (Anna Griffin); embroidery floss; vine pattern (source unknown); heart pattern (Embroidery on Paper by Design Originals)

There Is Always Love...

When accented with metal charms and used as page and photo mat borders, ribbons provided the perfect accents for this crisp father-son page. Here Andrea aligned green and blue ribbons and split, wove and criss-crossed them to create dynamic lines for added impact and attractive detail. Adorning the ribbons with tiny safety pins added an endearing infantile touch, while the bold patterned paper stripes and subtle stitching mimic Baby Nash's shirt. Andrea tied it all together with a letter sticker title, printed journaling strips and ink-treated metal frames.

Photos: Lifetouch/JC Penney, Aurora, Colorado

TECHNIQUE: To create her eye-catching ribbon borders, Andrea used tacky tape to help position and keep the ribbons in place, then machine stitched ed over ends that were pulled to the back of the page.

Supplies: Textured blue cardstock (Bazzill); patterned papers (Chatterbox); safety pins, ribbon charms, metal frames, alphabet stamps (Making Memories); alphabet stickers (Me & My Big Ideas); hands stamps (Inkadinkado); embroidery floss; ink

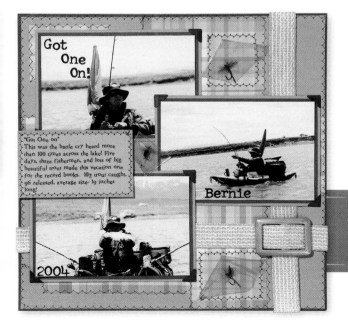

Got One On!

Andrea's page chronicling a successful fishing excursion was kept masculine and rustic with minimal accents, such as mica mounted with a fish hooks. Plaid patterned papers were stitched to the background page with green embroidery floss to pull in additional color, while bold strips of twill were inked and accented with a buckle at their intersection for a crisp look.

Supplies: Plaid patterned paper (Diane's Daughters); rub-on words (Making Memories); mica (USArtQuest); twill; buckle; blue and green cardstocks; green vellum; embroidery floss; fishing lure; photo corners; ink

TRICK: To highlight the fish hook embellishments, Andrea first mounted the mica over vellum and stitched along its edges to make the elements stand out against the background paper.

Heaven Sent

Plush yarn was used in place of traditional fibers for added texture. One segment was threaded through two rivets and tied with a charm, while two long segments span the height and width of the page and are joined by a tied piece at their intersection. The patterned paper was machine sewn to the background page while photo mats for the segmented and cropped photos were secured by backstitching through pierced holes. Double-matted printed journaling, metal corners and metal flower nails complete this elegant and understated page.

Photos: Lifetouch/JC Penney, Aurora, Colorado

TRICK: In using embroidery floss that is the same color as papers used in the layout, Andrea's stitching became a subtle element of the overall page design.

Supplies: Patterned paper, metal corners (Making Memories); rivets and flower nails (Chatterbox); cross charm (source unknown); embroidery floss; yarn scraps; vellum; ink; denim-colored cardstock

When Is a Weed Really a Flower?

Vibrant yellow rickrack interwoven with cropped photos helped to highlight the often-overlooked flowers celebrated in this layout. Andrea accomplished this look by cropping her photos and making eight 2" slices along one side of each photo. After mounting photos to the background, Andrea cut four 14" lengths of rickrack and wove three strips vertically between photos and one horizontally across the page, securing all ends with tacky tape.

TECHNIQUE: Notions needn't always be restricted to decorative page accents. Instead, feature them center stage as Andrea did here through the use of contrasting color and by employing eye-catching methods.

Supplies: Textured purple and lavender cardstocks (Bazzill); printed transparency sheet (Creative Imaginations); rickrack; brads

RUSH!
FREE ISSUE REQUEST!

BUSINESS REPLY MAIL
FIRST-CLASS MAIL   PERMIT NO. 347   FLAGLER BEACH FL

POSTAGE WILL BE PAID BY ADDRESSEE

MEMORY MAKERS
PO BOX 421400
PALM COAST FL 32142-7160

Eugene Lee Vetten

By making skilled artistic choices, Andrea artfully incorporated sewing and notions into a masculine layout. Subtle clusters of tiny buttons in the top page corners and bold rickrack borders kept the accents crisp and understated. When used to suspend frayed, ink-treated muslin scraps, sewing staples such as hooks and eyes became somewhat rugged and rustic hardware accents. Coupled with neatly stitched plaid and vintage-themed text patterned papers, this page exudes boyish charm all the while incorporating a delicate touch through Andrea's intricate handwork.

TECHNIQUE: Apart from artfully aging and distressing the muslin accents, the brown stamping ink and frayed ends evoke the fun Andrea enjoyed as a child playing with her brother in the dirt!

Supplies: Plaid patterned paper (Diane's Daughters); text patterned paper (Design Originals); alphabet stamps (Making Memories); muslin stickers (All My Memories); buttons; floss; brown ink; muslin scraps; rickrack; hook-and-eye closures

Have I Told You Lately...

Here several sepia photos and stitched patches of patterned paper combine for a quiltlike layout. Stitched hearts on frayed fabric squares lend a warm country feel. Hooks and eyes were used to suspend words and phrases cut from patterned paper while silk flower-adorned metal label holders provide charming accents. Finally, black photo corners and page corners provide a crisp finishing touch and air of nostalgia to the page.

TRICK: Andrea successfully blended country elements with modern accents by combining fabric swatches and a quilted background with trendy embellishments like label holders and label stickers.

Supplies: Patterned papers (Daisy D's, Diane's Daughters, Pressed Petals); metal label holders (Li'l Davis Designs); label stickers (Dymo); silk flowers; hooks and eyes; black photo corners; embroidery floss; stitched fabric hearts; frayed fabric squares; ribbon

Sharon WHITEHEAD

DESIGN DETAILS

Sharon first began scrapbooking in 1999 prior to the craft becoming a full-fledged "obsession" in 2002. With the addition of a computer, wide-format printer and scanner to her scrapbooking arsenal, Sharon found her niche and began creating pages enhanced by strategic design choices and purposeful page additions.

It's these smaller elements of page design working together that comprise Sharon's signature style. Especially fond of heritage photos, Sharon uses photo manipulation and accents to enhance the historical elements without having to use negatives or alter her precious heirlooms. "Details in design help set the mood, tell the story. Without the details it would just be another ordinary page. I want the photos to shine and for that design part of me to be there to share with my descendants even if I am not." While she credits technology as having revolutionized her approach to page design, Sharon also calls upon traditional design principles like placement, visual weight, repetition, symmetry, asymmetry, focus and rhythm, as well as incorporating concepts such as visual triangles and the rule of thirds. For Sharon, the notion of a little going a long way applies to page design. "Paying attention to details doesn't necessarily mean a complicated layout. It can be as simple as a sticker or die cut. It means paying attention to the mood, the message and the meaning of the photos to you."

Sharon lives in Vernon, British Columbia, Canada, with husband Paul. She has three children, son Stephen and daughters Kassandra and Lisa.

Beside Me Always

Here repetition was a key element in the success of Sharon's design. For a unique touch, the general shape and colors of the bridal bouquet were repeated using acrylic baubles layered over pieces of cut cardstock. The same colors were echoed throughout the layout in the title, select words of the journaling and also in the paint used to coat the metal word "always." Sharon also used the repetition of words throughout her journaling passage and again incorporated acrylic baubles into her title.

TECHNIQUE: Sharon printed her title twice to create the dimensional look, first directly onto the background page, then again onto paper. Select paper letters were then cut out and mounted over their corresponding letters with foam adhesive, some of which were coated with clear dimensional adhesive.

Supplies: Metal word, acrylic baubles (Making Memories); crystal lacquer (Sakura Hobby Craft); foam adhesive; acrylic paint

Happiness Is...

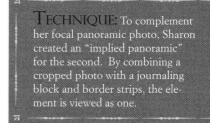

Several small details make this layout crisp and visually appealing. By keeping the strips and photos slightly shorter than the width of the background, Sharon created an implied border around the perimeter of the page. Square buttons threaded with embroidery floss in the color of the life jackets and border strips create a visual triangle, while horizontal placement of elements throughout the design add to the overall appeal.

Photos: Lisa Barth, Toronto, Ontario, Canada

TECHNIQUE: To complement her focal panoramic photo, Sharon created an "implied panoramic" for the second. By combining a cropped photo with a journaling block and border strips, the element is viewed as one.

Supplies: Textured blue-gray, light blue and bright peach cardstocks (Bazzill); square buttons (Making Memories); embroidery floss

Leap of Faith

This page is an example of an asymmetrical design with a one-third, two-thirds composition. This means most of the visual information is placed on the left side of the page. Sharon used the arrangement of her photos, burgundy accents and square brads to create visual triangles throughout the design, while the repetition of color and the placement of the text each add to the visual weight of the page.

TECHNIQUE: Sharon mimicked the shadow element of her computer-generated text by adding chalk detail to the focal photo mat and to the larger cross element.

Supplies: Textured gray and light blue cardstocks (Bazzill); square brads (Making Memories); charm (Blue Moon Beads); Print Master software (Broderbund); burgundy cardstock

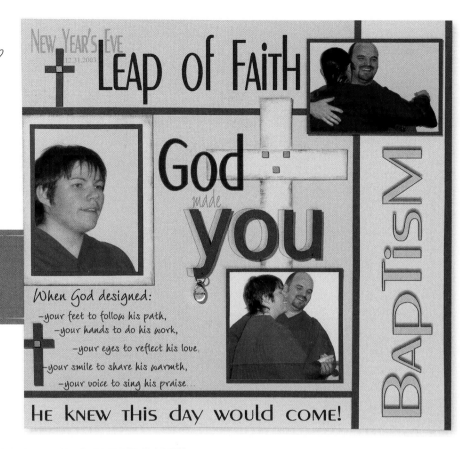

...Greetings from French Beach

Lots of little design details combine to complement this "picture-esque" page background. To create the look of a postcard, Sharon bordered her daughter alongside her sandy greeting with cardstock strips and a stamped and painted a foam element made to look like a postage stamp. A tag features a title created to mimic the look of breaking waves and is adorned further with seashells and ribbon.

TRICK: By enlarging and cropping a photo that had been taken from too far away, Sharon was able to make artful use of it as a background, which in turn captured all the detail.

Supplies: Textured mauve and blue-gray cardstocks (Bazzill); fun foam (Making Memories); alphabet stamps (Close To My Heart); heart die cut (Sizzix); acrylic paint, seashells

Family faces are magic mirrors

Looking at people who belong to us.
We see the past, present, and future.
-Gail Lumet Buckley

*Looking at you, I see the child you once
were, the young woman that you are
becoming, and the future that is yet to be for you.
I have to tell you that I miss that child you were
and thrill at getting to know better, the woman you
are becoming. I know that one day you will look back on
this day and wonder where all the time has gone.
Use it wisely, it goes by so quickly. I love you.
Summer 2002*

TRICK: To soften the edges of her metal photo corners and spiral accents, and to achieve a tightly rolled look, Sharon wrapped the elements around a mini turkey skewer.

Supplies: Metal mesh (Making Memories); watermark ink (Tsuki-neko); flower punches (EK Success, Marvy); silver and copper metal sheets; black cardstock; gold, copper and silver embossing powders; silver and copper brads; foam adhesive

Lisa

Sharon pulled the mirror element from the bottom photo and used it as inspiration for dictating the details of her design. A tiny mirror fragment was incorporated into a thematic quote, and several metal and embossed elements were used throughout as accents and to suggest the look of frames.

Punch flowers from copper foil.

Apply watermark ink to flowers and sprinkle with gold and silver embossing powder or extra thick embossing powder, leaving some of the copper exposed. Reapply as desired; heat to set.

Punch small flower for center of copper flower. Use a stylus to emboss center and curve petals for dimension.

Attach it to the center of the copper flower with faom adhesive. Shape petals of copper flower, reinforcing form with foam adhesive.

All the Art I Will Ever Need...

Sharon wanted an "artsy" feel to her page to illustrate a favorite quote and, simultaneously, her vision of her daughter. By mounting various metallic blocks on cardstock in stylish formations, Sharon was able to include her own artistic expression to emphasize her page theme. Square brass brads, hangers and curled copper page corners continue the metals theme and provide additional detail.

Supplies: Brass hangers (Victoria Art Supply Store); brass square brads and nailheads (www.scrapnpaper.com); suede paper, gold vellum (Paper Adventures); metallic copper paper (Jo-Ann Fabrics); gold paper; copper foil

TIP: For a simple way to create stark contrast and to emphasize select words, break the color scheme of your title by highlighting portions with foam-mounted white cardstock.

Glow By Night...

Placement, repetition and layering are the design details that light up this layout. Susan created block elements throughout her page starting with the background, which was done by covering white cardstock with various-sized sticky notes and removing them one at a time to fill the space with an acrylic paint and glaze mixture. Next Sharon repeated the use of blocks by devising an eye-appealing placement for each in layered configurations. Metal accents throughout add texture and visual balance.

Supplies: Metal mesh, hinges, copper snaps and eyelets (Making Memories); acrylic paint glaze (Golden Artist Colors); tag (Staples); Print Master software (Broderbund); labels (Dymo); acrylic paints; copper sheet; foam adhesive

TIP: Play with the placement of title text by changing the direction of select words for a dynamic, easy-to-achieve look.

Kin Folk

Each and every element of this heritage page was chosen for its timeless quality to be in keeping with a classic look. The texture of the handmade paper conjures images of crushed velvet draperies while tarnished-looking snaps, muted colors and the sepia-printed photo contribute to the feel of antiquity. A script font reminiscent of a woman's handwriting provided another striking detail to complement the page theme.

Supplies: Handmade paper (Victory Art Supply Store); corrugated paper (Timports); snaps (Welkmart); scrap copper foil; eyelets

TRICK: By repeating the use of torn handmade paper corner to corner across her photo mat, Sharon created balance paralleled by the larger torn section and instantly draws the eye across the photo.

Bold and Original

Bold and Original

Using her computer to add detail and enhance her design is one of Sharon's favorite techniques, and this bold and graphic page is a prime example. Here manipulated text in various fonts span the page and focal photo. Punched daisies reflect the sticker featured on Sharon's daughter's sunglasses and provide fun and funky detail. Susan used computer software to determine the placement of her photos and text, making adjustments and printing test sheets before committing the design to her background paper.

TIP: Conduct a key word search by typing "free fonts" on your search engine to discover sites that feature free downloadable fonts. Soon you'll have a wealth of typographical options at your fingertips.

Supplies: Textured green cardstock (Bazzill); watermark ink (Tsukineko); Print Master Gold 12 software (Broderbund); brads; eyelets; embossing powder

---

Trust

Sharon enhanced what were originally photos with distracting backgrounds to become shots deserving of center stage. She scanned the photos in color and layered each with a black-and-white version, then used the erasure tool to edit the black-and-white layer. In so doing, only the desired elements of the colored layer were revealed. Once cropped and assembled into a collage, Sharon added flower accents to provide a punch of extra color and contrast.

TIP: When creating a photo collage, eliminate busy backgrounds with editing software to create a visually appealing grouping. Watch out for trapped white space, keep accents to a minimum and include an identifiable focal photo.

Supplies: Textured orange cardstock (Bazzill); leather flowers (Making Memories); ribbon; buttons

from ***Simple beginnings...*** there are very few photos of my mother growing up. Her parents were poor farmers on the Canadian prairies. The land was theirs but there was little money. Seeing this child, in her roughly cut, flour sack dress. tugs at my heart. She had told me of the harsh existence growing up on the farm, but the photos say so much more. Her clothing was often bleached flour sacks or hand-me-downs from her four older sisters.

Virginia, age 10, 1936

Virginia, age 4, 1930

Smith
FAMILY
MEMORIES

Virginia, age 4, 1930

Virginia, age 2; Prince; Terry, age 4 - 1928

Simple Beginnings

Here again technology was called upon to enhance the historical detail of an heirloom photo, which was printed in sepia and enlarged for the background. Three additional photos pop from the page with the use of double mats and photo corners. A simple font continued the understated theme while rub-ons, diagonally cut mesh, a paper flower and cardstock stickers provide rustic detail. A paint-altered "V" added a subtle touch in honor of Sharon's mother's name.

TRICK: With the incorporation of the dusty-rose colored cardstock mats, Sharon's secondary photos were given emphasis to bring out the visual triangle created by their placement. Moreover, the color makes for an attractive addition to the layout's muted hues.

Supplies: Rub-ons, metal "V," oversized brad, paper flower (Making Memories); mini brads (www.scrapnpaper.com); mesh (Magic Mesh); cardstock stickers (Pebbles); acrylic paint; hinge

Celebrate Your Spirit

A special photo of Sharon's aunt playing dress-up inspired this rough-around-the-edges, albeit elegant page. To emphasize the title, Sharon used various fonts, sizes and colors. Metal hinges and a label holder provide rustic detail and were altered with paint and sanding. Dry-brush painting and sanding made for rugged borders along the edges of the photo and perimeter of the page for an appealing frame effect.

TECHNIQUE: Easily add rugged beauty and texture to any page design with touches of paint, sanding and paper curling.

Supplies: Photo flips, label holder, antique copper brads (Making Memories); dusty rose-colored cardstock; acrylic paint

Auntie Ruth, a smile tugging at her lips as she looked at this old photo, commented wistfully that dressing up in her mom's old treasures was one of her favorite pastimes as a child. She never noticed that they were old and worn or that the shoes were too big. **In that moment, no greater princess there ever was.** As a child she saw herself as beautiful and stylish, just like her mom and older sisters. So, Auntie Ruth, celebrate your spirit. The spirit of the little girl that still resides within you ~July 2004

celebrate
your *Spirit*
in
Style

Auntie Ruth
1939

Now and Forever

Sharon adorned her enlarged photo with a mini book containing an additional photo and journaling in the style of her page background. Circles, strips, mitered borders and brad accents were repeated on each, as was the use of rub-on titles.

TECHNIQUE: Create a unified look between pages in the same album by making your own "patterned papers" using cardstock strips and shapes in various colors and widths.

Supplies: Text patterned paper (7 Gypsies); metal flower, snaps, rub-ons, mini brads (Making Memories); hinges (found at local hardware store)

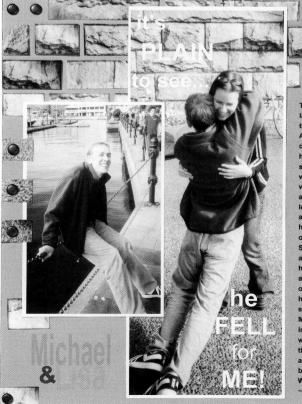

That's what you told me, laughingly, as you showed me the proof of the photo. Actually, the photo was taken during a walk to the inner harbour in Victoria, their favorite spot for walking. Occasionally when Michael gives Lisa a hug, without warning he goes absolutely limp in her arms, leaving her giggling and hardly able to hold him up. It is evident how much they really enjoy each other.
So, when my daughter recently announced that he had asked her to marry him and she had accepted, her father and I were overjoyed for them. If we could have picked anyone for a son-in-law, it would have been Michael. From the day we were introduced to him we knew there was something special between them. Their engagement came as no surprise and we couldn't be happier.
Welcome to the family, Michael!
~photo taken April/2004

It's Plain To See...

Sharon made artful use of her focal photo's background elements in this fun and romantic layout. By using her computer to print extra copies of the brick background, Sharon was able to cut out the blocks and mount several with foam adhesive. In addition to producing an eye-appealing effect, the symbolic notion of building a strong foundation in this young relationship is represented. For a subtle touch, circle brads lend additional shape to an otherwise linear page.

TRICK: Enlarge and crop ordinary photos to create the look of a vertical panoramic photo as a striking means to fill page space and enhance the subject.

Supplies: Textured lavender cardstock (Bazzill); brads; foam adhesive

…That Pesce Trait

A corner rounder and cropped cardstock elements were used to define spaces and create implied lines in this layout. Once Sharon arranged her text using computer software to accommodate the cropped and rounded photos, rounded cardstock pieces were incorporated to enclose the space. Paint-altered molding, leather flowers and ribbon details incorporate colors from the focal photo for nice finishing touches.

Photos: FoxFish Photography, Arvada, Colorado

TRICK: Create complex-looking designs that come together quickly with pre-planned arrangement aided by your computer.

Supplies: Textured blue and pink cardstocks (Bazzill); Print Master Gold 12 software (Broderbund); molding strips, molding corners, leather flowers, oversized brads (Making Memories); paper charms (Pebbles); corner rounder (Marvy); ribbon; acrylic paint

CHIARA'S got that **pesce** trait

Grandpa Pesce, Daddy, and Anna did it. Now Chiara does it too. Evidently the **TONGUE** is an important part of a Pesce's anatomy, especially when concentrating or deep in thought.

Chiara almost always has a tip of her tongue **STICKING OUT** while sleeping. Even when awake, inevitably it's sticking out and can be seen in most photos. another tidbit, re: THE PESCE TONGUES - both girls suck on their tongues while sleeping.

SHE USES HER TONGUE AS HER OWN 'PERSONAL PACIFIER'

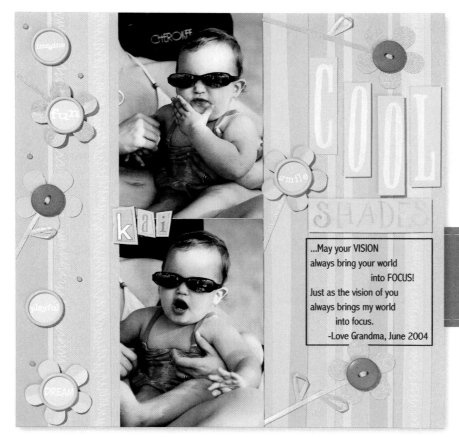

imagine / fun / smile / kai / playful / DREAM / CHEROKEE / **COOL SHADES**

...May your VISION always bring your world into FOCUS! Just as the vision of you always brings my world into focus. -Love Grandma, June 2004

Cool Shades

Using several elements from the same line of product helped Sharon create this bright and bold design. In addition to adding instant eye-appeal, the various embellishments carry the eye smoothly over the layout all the while complementing the fun photos. A stamped and foam adhesive-mounted title provided another tactile element while the computer-printed journaling block helped ground the layout for good measure.

TRICK: By simply folding her paper flower petals in half for dimension and by adding buttons or concho centers and ribbon stems, Sharon easily took her punched flower accents to the next level.

Supplies: Patterned paper, word punch-outs, studs, conchos (Scrapworks); alphabet stamps (Making Memories); acrylic alphabet stamps (Close To My Heart); watermark ink (Tsukineko); flower punch (EK Success); cardstock stickers (Pebbles); buttons; chalk; acrylic paint; ribbon

Additional Instructions and Credits

VINTAGE SUMMER P.6

For an artful addition to an endearing photo, Joanna printed her journaling onto a transparency, cut it to size, layered it over a piece of vellum and then adhered the two sheets over the photo with a decorative paper clip. By adding the vellum layer between the photo and the journaling, the photo can still be seen but the journaling is more legible against the softer, muted image. Additionally, Joanna created two packing tape transfers from truck-patterned paper by applying the tape to a color copy of the desired image, burnishing to ensure adhesion. She then removed the tape from the paper and wet it with warm water, then rubbed gently to work the paper off of the sticky side of the tape. The first transfer was mounted at the top left corner of the page and the second was trimmed and mounted beneath a leather frame. She then layered the frame with a section cut from a printed transparency and applied a rub-on word.

Supplies: Patterned papers, file folder (Rusty Pickle); leather frame, leather flower (Making Memories); printed transparency (Daisy D's); decorative paper clip (EK Success); rub-on word (Autumn Leaves); transparency; red cardstock

PARK PLAY P.18

Vibrant cardstock circles stacked in graduated fashion form a whimsical page border and instantly add depth to this fun design. To bring in a little shine and extra dimension, Jennifer added page pebble centers to three of the four circle accents. Bold border strips and circle-cut journaling complete this playful page.

Supplies: Textured green, royal blue, light blue, red, orange, peach and yellow cardstocks (Bazzill); label holder (Magic Scraps); page pebbles (K & Company); dimensional adhesive (JudiKins); alphabet stamps (PSX Design); stamping ink; brads; light green, white and orange papers

MY FUNNY VALENTINE P.30

Susan uses a double-entendre of "Funny Valentine" to refer to both her husband and the valentine she made for him, which is displayed in a pocket made from a transparency and brads. Silly outtakes from a photo shoot provided the perfect complement to Susan's page theme. Playing cards from the suit of hearts are fun and symbolic additions, as Susan's husband is the "king" of her heart and eight is the number of years they have been together. Bright colors and whimsical patterns and accents add additional punch to this punchy page.

Supplies: Patterned paper (KI Memories); oversized brads (Hyglo); stickers (Paper House Productions); metal word (Making Memories); slide holders (DMD); letter stamps (FontWerks); watermark ink (Tsukineko); orange and white cardstocks; transparency; playing cards; pen; chalk

JERSEY GIRLS P.42

Intrigued by a favorite family heritage photo that offered little insight regarding date and occasion, Lisa let her imagination speculate the photo's story. Knowing only identities, Lisa approximated the year based on clues such as clothing and drew upon recollections of personalities and family stories to imagine a situation for her journaling. Printing words on vellum and transparencies incorporates additional journaling details in a subtle fashion.

Supplies: Patterned papers, slide mounts, colored transparency (Design Originals); printable canvas (Burlington); clear transparency; vellum; various inks; brads; sand and seashells

RECESSIVE BLUE GENES P.54

Inspired by her son's striking blue eyes, Kathy created a layout that cleverly combines the recessive genotype for blue eye color (bb) with all-blue page elements. Kathy began by placing emphasis on Isaac's eyes by removing the other colors from the photo using a image-editing program. Combining a range of blues with black and white created a rich monochromatic color scheme where Kathy used stamping, chalking, papers, letter stickers, tags, fibers, computer font journaling and even blue staples to comprise her true blue layout.

Supplies: Text patterned paper (Carolee's Creations); crackle patterned paper (source unknown); wire mesh, date stamp, staples (Making Memories); letter stamps (Printworks, PSX Design, Wordsworth); metal-rimmed tags, silver brads (Treasured Memories); blue tags (Designer's Library); black letter stickers (Wordsworth); blue letter stickers (Chatterbox); denim letter stickers (Karen Foster Design); blue tiles (EK Success); fibers; ink; blue and black cardstocks and papers

LOVE P.66

This darling photo of Angie's daughter in a log cabin conjured images of a little Laura Ingalls Wilder. Consequently, she was inspired to include a quote from the famous pioneer on a tag that was then slipped inside a small paper bag. The handwritten tag was inked and tied off with a strip of fabric. Lace trim, an epoxy sticker and a silk flower with a decorative brad center adorn the bag.

Supplies: Patterned papers (Karen Foster Design, Daisy D's, Paper Co.); "love" sticker (Sweetwater); paper bag (DMD); epoxy sticker (K & Company.); decorative brad (Making Memories); pen, chalk ink, fabric striop, silk flower, tag

ESSENCE OF SPRING P.78

Michelle used multiple fonts and sizes to complement her collage-style layout. The first three words of the title were printed onto vellum. "Spring" was printed in reverse, temporarily adhered to black cardstock, then cut with a craft knife. A typewriter style font was chosen for the border words to make them resemble labels. These were printed in the same font as "essence" in the title to pull the elements together. Michelle's own handwriting comprises the vellum journaling blocks.

Supplies: Patterned papers (Club Scrap, Colors By Design, Hot Off The Press, K & Company, Making Memories); stamps (Club Scrap, Hero Arts, Stamps by Judith); paper-piecing pattern (Carson-Dellosa); transparency words, printed transparency, slide mounts (LeaveMemories); dimensional pearl paint (Ranger); dried flowers (Pressed Petals); punched flowers, flower sticker (EK Success); dimensional adhesive (JudiKins); snaps (Making Memories); tiny glass beads (Magic Scraps); pansy cutouts (Hot Off The Press); corrugated paper (Club Scrap); vellum; tissue; mini eyelets; pen; chalk; colored pencil; foam adhesive; decoupage adhesive; ink; embossing powder; dried flower petals; snaps

ONE PRECIOUS FACE P.90

This layout is as rich in texture as autumn is in color. Denise layered script patterned paper with embossed strips that have been treated with acrylic paint, metallic rub-ons and accented with rivets. Shell leaf pendants mounted over glossy mica cascade down the page, adding a smooth, shiny texture. The frayed ends of cardstock-mounted and shaded aida cloth lends yet another tactile element. Strategic use of foam adhesive contributes to the dimension Denise created in the page.

Supplies: Patterned paper (Design Originals); embossed papers (Provo Craft); shell leaf pendants (Beadery); mica (ArtChix); metal corner (Eggery Place); rivets (Chatterbox); metallic rub-ons (Craf-T); aida cloth (DMC); brads; acrylic paint

BAREFOOT IN BLUE JEANS P.102

In addition to a denim-patterned paper background, Andrea incorporated the real thing for especially fun accents. Frayed denim swatches, a pocket, overall straps and snap-centered silk flowers make an eye-catching combination that perfectly complements the photo. Border stitching, buttons and hand sewn flower title accents complete the look.

Photo: Lifetouch/JC Penney, Aurora, Colorado

Supplies: Denim patterned paper (Karen Foster Design); alphabet stamps (Making Memories, Stampabilities); buttons (Jesse James); denim overall elements; silk flowers; snaps; embroidery floss; eyelets; fibers; beads

MY UNCLE FRED P.114

Striking detail and dimension are added to this heritage-themed layout by individually mounting stamped and sticker letters onto cardstock mats. Sharon created additional visual interest by mounting several of the elements with foam adhesive and adorning with small accents like spiral clips and ball chains. Paper tearing lends itself well to the rugged layout, and is given a unique twist by curling the edges around a large turkey skewer for appealing page corners. By enlarging her photo, Sharon was able to include the barn in the distance that would have otherwise been lost.

Supplies: Label holder (Staples); mini brads (Jo-Ann Fabrics); stamps (Hero Arts, Making Memories); watermark ink (Tsukineko); spiral clips (Making Memories); ball chains (Westrim); "grow" stamp (Close To My Heart); stickers (Pebbles); ink; chalk; fibers

Source guide

The following companies manufacture products featured in this book. Please check your local retailers to find these materials, or go to a company's Web site for the latest product. In addition, we have made every attempt to properly credit the items mentioned in this book. We apologize to any company that we have listed incorrectly, and we would appreciate hearing from you.

2DYE4
www.canscrapink.com
7 Gypsies
(800) 588-6707
www.7gypsies.com
Adobe
www.adobe.com
All My Memories
(888) 553-1998
www.allmymemories.com
All Night Media
(see Plaid Enterprises)
American Art Clay Co. (AMACO)
(800) 374-1600
www.amaco.com
American Crafts
(801) 2226-0747
www.americancrafts.com
American Typewriter - no contact info
Ampersand Art Supply
(800) 822-1939
www.ampersandart.com
Amscan, Inc.
(800) 444-8887
www.amscan.com
Amy's - no contact info
Anima Designs
(800) 570-6847
www.animadesigns.com
Anna Griffin, Inc.
(wholesale only)
(888) 817-8170
www.annagriffin.com
Arcsoft - no contact info
ARTchix Studio
(250) 370-9985
www.artchixstudio.com
Artistic Expressions
(219) 764-5158
www.artisticexpressionsinc.com
Artistic Scrapper
www.artisticscrapper.com
Autumn Leaves (wholesale only)
(800) 588-6707
www.autumnleaves.com

Avery Dennison Corporation
(800) GO-AVERY
www.avery.com
Bag of Beach - no contact info
Basic Grey™
(801) 451-6006
www.basicgrey.com
Bazzill Basics Paper
(480) 558-8557
www.bazzillbasics.com
Beadery®, The
(401) 539-2432
www.thebeadery.com
Blue Moon Beads
(800) 377-6715
www.bluemoonbeads.com
Bo-Bunny Press
(801) 771-4010
www.bobunny.com
Boutique Trims, Inc.
(248) 437-2017
www.boutiquetrims.com
Boxer Scrapbook Productions
(888) 625-6255
www.boxerscrapbooks.com
Broderbund Software
(319) 247-3325
www.broderbund.com
Burlington - no contact info
Canson®, Inc.
(800) 628-9283
www.canson-us.com
Card Connection - see Michaels
CARL Mfg. USA, Inc.
(800) 257-4771
www.Carl-Products.com
Carolee's Creations®
(435) 563-1100
www.ccpaper.com
Carson-Dellosa Publishing Co.
(800) 321-0943
www.carsondellosa.com
Charles Craft - no contact info
Chatterbox, Inc.
(208) 939-9133
www.chatterboxinc.com
Clearsnap, Inc.
(360) 293-6634
www.clearsnap.com
Clipiola - no contact info
Close To My Heart®
(888) 655-6552
www.closetomyheart.com
Cloud 9 Design
(763) 493-0990
www.cloud9design.biz
Club Scrap™, Inc.
(888) 634-9100
www.clubscrap.com
Cock-A-Doodle Design, Inc.
(800) 954-0559
www.cockadoodledesign.com
Colorbök™, Inc. (wholesale only)
(800) 366-4660
Colors by Design
(800) 832-8436
www.colorsbydesign.com
Craf-T Products
(507) 235-3996
www.craf-tproducts.com
Crafts, Etc. Ltd.
(800) 888-0321
www.craftsetc.com
Create A Craft - no contact info
Creative Imaginations
(800) 942-6487
www.cigift.com
Creative Impressions Rubber Stamps, Inc.
(719) 596-4860
www.creativeimpressions.com
Creative Memories®
(800) 468-9335
www.creativememories.com
Creek Bank Creations, Inc.
(217) 427-5980
www.creekbankcreations.com
C-Thru® Ruler Company, The
Wholesale only)
(800) 243-8419
www.cthruruler.com
Current®, Inc.
(800) 848-2848
www.currentinc.com
Daisy D's Paper Company
(888) 601-8955
www.daisydspaper.com
Darice, Inc.
(800_ 321-1494
www.darice.com
Delta Technical Coatings, Inc.
(800) 423-4135
www.deltacrafts.com
Deluxe Designs
(480) 205-9210
www.deluxedesigns.com
Deluxe Plastic Arts - no contact info
DeNami Design Rubber Stamps
(253) 437-1626
www.denamidesign.com
Derwent Cumberland Pencil Co.
www.pencils.co.uk
Design Originals
(800) 877-0067
www.d-originals.com

Designer's Library by Lana, The
(660) 582-6484
www.thedesignerslibrary.com
Diane's Daughters®
(801) 621-8392
www.dianesdaughters.com
DiBona Designs
(888) 685-5538
www.dibonadesigns.com
DMC Corp.
(973) 589-0606
www.dmc.com
DMD Industries, Inc.
(Wholesale only)
(800) 805-9890
www.dmdind.com
Doodlebug Design™ Inc.
(801) 966-9952
www.doodlebugdesigninc.com
Duncan Enterprises
(800) 782-6748
www.duncan-enterprises .com
Dymo
www.dymo.com
Eggery Place, The
www.theeggeryplace.com
EK Success™, Ltd.
(Wholesale only)
(800) 524-1349
www.eksuccess.com
Emagination Crafts, Inc.
(Wholesale only)
(630) 833-9521
www.emaginationcrafts.com
Esselte®
www.esselte.com
Expo International - no contact info
Family Archives™, The
(888) 622-6556
www.heritagescrapbooks.com
Family Treasures, Inc.®
www.familytreasures.com
Flair® Designs
(888) 546-9990
www.flairdesignsinc.com
FontWerks
www.fontwerks.com
FoofaLa
(402) 758-0863
www.foofala.com
Frances Meyer, Inc.®
(800) 372-6237
www.francesmeyer.com
Freckle Press - no contact info
Fuji Photo Film U.S.A., Inc.
(800) 755-3854
www.fujifilm.com
Gaylord Bros.
(800) 634-6307
www.gaylord.com
Gerber
(800) 4-GERBER
www.gerber.com
Golden Artist Colors, Inc.
(800) 959-6543
www.goldenpaints.com
Grafix®
(800) 447-2349
www.grafix.com
Hasbro®
www.hasbro.com
Heartland Crafts - no contact info
Hero Arts® Rubber Stamps, Inc.
(800) 822-4376
www.heroarts.com
Hewlett-Packard Company
www.hp.com
Hirschberg Schutz & Co., Inc.
(800) 221-8640
Hobby Lobby Stores, Inc.
www.hobbylobby.com
Home Depot U.S.A., Inc.
www.homedepot.com
Hot Off The Press, Inc.
(800) 227-9595
www.paperpizazz.com
Hot Potatoes
(615) 296-8002
www.hotpotatoes.com
Hunt Corporation
(800) 879-4868
www.hunt-corp.com
HyGlo®/American Pin
(480) 968-6475
www.hyglocrafts.com
Hy-Ko Products
(800) 292-0550
www.hy-ko.com
Imagination Project, Inc.
(513) 860-2711
www.imaginationproject.com
Impress Rubber Stamps
(206) 901-9101
www.impressrubberstamps.com
Inkadinkado® Rubber Stamps
(800) 888-4652
www.inkadinkado.com
Jane, Inc. - no contact info
Jesse James & Co., Inc.
(610) 435-0201
www.jessejamesbutton.com
Jest Charming
(702) 564-5101
www.jestcharming.com

JHB International
(303) 751-8100
www.buttons.com
Jo-Ann Fabric & Crafts
(888) 739-4120
www.joann.com
JudiKins
(310) 515-1115
www.judikins.com
Junkitz™
(732) 792-1108
www.junkitz.com
K & Company
(888) 244-2083
www.kandcompany.com
Karen Foster Design
(Wholesale only)
(801) 451-9779
www.karenfosterdesign.com
Karen's Crafts - no contact info
Keeping Memories Alive™
(800) 419-4949
www.scrapbooks.com
Keller's Creations (wholesale only)
(706) 736-6450
www.acidfree.com
KI Memories
(972) 243-5595
www.kimemories.com
Kopp Design
(801) 489-6011
www.koppdesign.com
Krylon®
(216) 566-200
www.krylon.com
Lakeshore Learning Materials
(800) 421-5354
www.lakeshorelearning.com
Lasting Impressions for Paper, Inc.
(801) 298-1979
www.lastingimpressions.com
Leave Memories
(518)281-4393
www.leavememories.com
Lee Valley Tools, Ltd.
(800) 871-8158
www.leevalley.com
Leeco Industries, Inc.
(800) 826-8806
www.leecoindustries.com
Li'l Davis Designs
(949) 838-0344
www.lildavisdesigns.com
Limited Edition Rubberstamps
(650) 594-4242
www.limitededitionrs.com
Liquitex® Artist Materials
(888) 4-ACRYLIC
www.liquitex.com
LuminArte (formerly Angelwing Enterprises)
(866) 229-1544
www.luminarteinc.com
Ma Vinci's Reliquary
http://crafts.dm.net/
mall/reliquary/
Magenta Rubber Stamps
(Wholesale only)
(800) 565-5254
www.magentastyle.com
Magic Mesh
(651) 345-6374
www.magicmesh.com
Magic Scraps™
(972) 238-1838
www.magicscraps.com
Magnetic Poetry®
(800) 370-7697
www.magneticpoetry.com
Making Memories
(800) 286-5263
www.makingmemories.com
Marvy® Uchida/ Uchida of America, Corp.
(800) 541-5877
www.uchida.com
me & My BiG ideas®
(wholesale only)
(949) 883-2065
www.meandmybigideas.com
Memories Complete™, LLC
(866) 966-6365
www.memoriescomplete.com
Meri Meri
www.merimeri.com
Michaels® Arts & Crafts
(800) 642-4235
www.michaels.com
MOD-my own design
(303) 641-8680
www.mod-myowndesign.com
Moore - no contact info
Mosaic Mercantile
(877) 9-MOSAIC
www.mosaicmercantile.com
Moto Photo
(800) 454-6686
www.motophoto.com
Mrs. Grossman's Paper Company
(Wholesale only)
(800) 429-4549
www.mrsgrossmans.com
Mustard Moon™
(408) 299-8542
www.mustardmoon.com

My Mind's Eye™, Inc.
(801) 298-3709
www.frame-ups.com
National Cardstock - no longer in business
Nature's Pressed
(800) 850-2499
www.naturespressed.com
Neenah Paper, Inc.
(678) 566-6500
www.neenah.com
Nicole - no contact info
Office Depot
www.officedepot.com
Offray
www.offray.com
Paper Adventures®
(800) 727-0699
www.paperadventures.com
Paper Co., The/ANW Crestwood
(800) 525-3196
www.anwcrestwood.com
Paper House Productions®
(800) 255-7316
www.paperhouseproductions.com
Paper Loft
(801) 446-7249
www.paperloft.com
Paperbilities - no contact info
Parker Metal Corporation
www.parkermetal.com
Pebbles Inc.
(801) 224-1857
www.pebblesinc.com
Pier 1 Imports®
(800) 245-4595
www.pier1.com
Pioneer Photo Albums, Inc.®
(800) 366-3686
www.pioneerphotoalbums.com
Plaid Enterprises, Inc.
(800) 842-4197
www.plaidonline.com
Polyform Products Co.
(847) 427-0020
www.sculpey.com
Pressed Petals
(800) 748-4656
www.pressedpetals.com
Prima
(909) 627-5532
www.mulberrypaperflowers.com
PrintWorks
(800) 854-6558
www.printworks.com
Provo Craft® (Wholesale only)
(888) 577-3545
www.provocraft.com
Prym-Dritz Corporation
www.dritz.com
PSX Design™
(800) 782-6748
www.psxdesign.com
QuickKutz
(801) 765-1144
www.quickkutz.com
Ranger Industries, Inc.
(800) 244-2211
www.rangerink.com
River City Rubber Works
(877) 735-2276
www.rivercityrubberworks.com
Rocky Mountain Scrapbook Co.
(801) 785-9695
www.rmscrapbook.com
Rollabind LLC
(800) 438-3542
www.rollabind.com
Royal® & Langnickel/Royal Brush Mfg.
(219) 660-4170
www.royalbrush.com
Rusty Pickle
(801) 272-2280
www.rustypickle.com
Sakura Hobby Craft
(310) 212-7878
www.sakuracraft.com
Sandylion Sticker Designs
(800) 387-4215
www.sandylion.com
Saral Paper Corp.
(212) 223-3322
www.saralpaper.com
Scenic Route Paper Co.
(801) 785-0761
www.scenicroutepaper.com
Scrap Ease®
(800) 272-3874
www.whatsnewltd.com
Scrap in a Snap™
(513) 829-6610
www.scrapinasnap.com
Scrap Pagerz™
(435) 645-0696
www.scrappagerz.com
Scrapbook Wizard™, The
(435) 752-7555
www.scrapbookwizard.com
Scrapheap Re³
www.canscrapink.com

Scrappy Cat™, LLC
(440) 234-4850
www.scrappycatcreations.com
ScrapTherapy Designs, Inc.
(800) 333-7880
www.scraptherapy.com
Scrapworks, LLC
(801) 363-1010
www.scrapworks.com
Scrapyard 329
(775) 829–1118
www.scrayard329.com
SEI, Inc.
(800) 333-3279
www.shopsei.com
Sizzix®
(866) 742-4447
www.sizzix.com
Sonburn, Inc.
(800) 527-7505
www.sonburn.com
S.R.M. Press, Inc.
(800) 323-9589
www.srmpress.com
Stamp Craft - see Plaid Enterprises
Stampabilities®
(800) 888-0321
www.stampabilities.com
Stampendous!®
(800) 869-0474
www.stampendous.com
Stamper's Choice - no contact info
Stampin' Up!®
(800) 782-6787
www.stampinup.com
Stamping Station
(801) 444-3828
www.stampingstation.com
Stampington & Company
(877) STAMPER
www.stampington.com
Stamps by Judith
www.stampsbyjudith.com
Staples, Inc.
(800) 3STAPLE
www.staples.com
Stewart Superior Corporation
(800) 558-2875
www.stewartsuperior.com
Sticker Studio™
(208) 322-2465
www.stickerstudio.com
Sweetwater
(800) 359-3094
www.sweetwaterscrapbook.com
SWIBCO, Inc.
(630) 968-8900
www.swibco.com
Tandy - no contact info
Target
www.target.com
Teacher Supply Store - no contact info
Tejas Lace Company - no contact info
Therm O Web, Inc.
(800) 323-0799
www.thermoweb.com
Timeless Touches™/Dove Valley Productions, LLC
(623) 362-8285
www.timelesstouches.net
Timports - no contact info
Treasured Memories - no contact info
Tsukineko®, Inc.
(800) 769-6633
www.tsukineko.com
Tumblebeasts LLC
(505) 323-5554
www.tumblebeasts.com
Tumbleweed - no contact info
Unique Boutiques - no contact info
U.S. Shell, Inc.
(956) 943-1709
www.usshell.com
USArtQuest, Inc.
(517) 522-6225
www.usartquest.com
Victoria Art Supply Store - no contact info
Victorian Paper Company/Victorian Trading Co.
www.victoriantrading.com
VWR™ International
(800) 932-5000
www.vwr.com
Wal-Mart Stores, Inc.
(800) WALMART
www.walmart.com
Walnut Hollow® Farm, Inc.
(800) 950-5101
www.walnuthollow.com
Welkmart - no contact info
Westrim® Crafts
(800) 727-2727
www.westrimcrafts.com
Wordsworth
(719) 282-3495
www.wordsworthstamps.com
Wrights® Ribbon Accents
(877) 597-4448
www.wrights.com

Index